Selection and Control

Teachers' Ratings of Children in the Infant School

Primary Socialization, Language and Education
Edited by Basil Bernstein
University of London Institute of Education
Sociological Research Unit

I *Social Class, Language and Communication*
W. Brandis & D. Henderson

II *A Linguistic Description and Computer Program for Children's Speech*
G. J. Turner & B. A. Mohan

III *Talk Reform*
D. M. & G. A. Gahagan

IV *Class, Codes and Control*
Volume 1 *Theoretical Studies towards a Sociology of Language*
Volume 2 *Applied Studies towards a Sociology of Language*
B. Bernstein

V *A Question of Answers* (*2 vols*)
W. P. Robinson & S. J. Rackstraw

VI *Social Control and Socialization*
J. Cook-Gumperz

A catalogue of other series of Social Science books published by Routledge & Kegan Paul will be found at the end of this volume.

Selection and Control

Teachers' Ratings of Children in the Infant School

Walter Brandis and
Basil Bernstein

Sociological Research Unit
University of London Institute of Education

ROUTLEDGE & KEGAN PAUL
London and Boston

First published in 1974
by Routledge & Kegan Paul Ltd
Broadway House, 68–74 Carter Lane,
London EC4V 5EL and
9 Park Street,
Boston, Mass. 02108, USA
Printed in Great Britain by
Clarke, Doble & Brendon Ltd
Plymouth

ISBN 0 7100 7729 7

Library of Congress Catalog Card No. 73-87313

Contents

Preface

This monograph consists of an analysis of teachers' ratings of children in a middle-class and in a working-class area at the end of their first year and at the end of their second year of life in the infant school. The Appendix presents the results of sections of an interview with the mothers of the children which took place about four months before the children entered the infant school. We have previously published results of other sections of this interview (Bernstein and Young, 1967; Brandis and Bernstein, 1970; Robinson and Rackstraw, 1972; Cook-Gumperz, 1973). In this Appendix we present our analysis of the mothers' tape-recorded replies to open-ended questions which focused upon the preparation of children for the experience of the infant school. We should also point out that when the mothers were interviewed two and a half years later for the second time, we covered some of the areas of the first interview. When these results are published it will be seen that they broadly confirm the findings of the first interview.

We have had some difficulty in deciding how to present the two major parts of this monograph. The crucial section is Part I but this is highly technical, and necessarily so, as it sets out in some detail the logic of the statistical description. Inasmuch as the form of the reasoning places it beyond the reach of those who are not specialists, then the reasoning is not open to *general* criticism. On the other hand, if the assumptions and procedures are not made explicit then there we have a 'popular' account which makes it difficult for the approach to be subject to *any* informed criticism. Part I contains both the method *and* the major findings. Part II is much less technical and it is *one* interpretation of the findings as these might throw light upon differences in the patterns of the teachers' judgments in the middle-class and in the working-class area. This interpretation clearly can be criticised in its own right, but the imputed patterns are derived from findings created by the analysis in Part I. It may be that popular accounts of some research should be written only after the more specialised accounts have been subject to criticism. This is not a disguised argument for limiting research activities to researchers, neither does it involve any necessarily invidious relationship between researcher, researched and general reader; it is simply a recognition of the problems entailed in social research into areas of general interest and public concern.

There are problems about the kinds of inferences which can be made from the data constructed by any approach in the social sciences, and the approach in this monograph is no exception. Indeed, data which presume directly to reflect people, their experience and their realities often rest upon veiled assumptions, upon tacit classifications and frames which are the unspoken, silent ground of the project. In our case, our data is limited in the following respects. We have no direct observation of the teachers and children which can serve as a check on the ratings. We have created the criteria and scales the teachers used to rate the children.[1] We do not know what counts for any teacher as 'co-operative', 'attentive' and so on. We know little about each individual teacher, except her qualifications, age, teaching experience and the length of time she taught in each LEA. The two groups of teachers show very similar patterns of variation with respect to each of these characteristics. To obtain extended knowledge of the above would require a major research activity in its own right; whereas for us this particular enquiry was one of a series of enquiries within a programme whose major focus was elsewhere. Furthermore, even if we had wished to employ a more sensitive approach, we did not have either the time or the resources and, of more importance, we had imposed upon the teachers' time in so many other ways that we, quite rightly, may well have had difficulty in obtaining co-operation. This report is therefore exploratory and we hope suggestive.

Studies of this type do, however, draw attention to aspects of teacher-pupil relationships which may be more reliably investigated by observing actual behaviour. For example, there are suggestions that girls are likely to be viewed more favourably than boys; that teachers may be more sensitive to analogical reasoning in the middle-class area than in the working-class area; that self-regulatory behaviour is a more important component of the set of ratings in the middle-class area than in the working-class area; that although girls are rated 'brighter' than boys, there is a hint that they are likely to receive a less favourable school prognosis than boys; that a polarisation of children in terms of ability test scores occurs in the first years of the infant school, and this is more pronounced in the working-class area; that an assessment of *reported* maternal communication has an increasing relationship with the teachers' assessment of the child's verbal behaviour in the classrooms; that middle-class children's non-verbal ability scores (WISC) have little or no relationship to a favourable teacher's estimate; that despite variations between teachers and despite the current ideology of the infant school, it is the measured ability of the infant-school child which has the strongest relation to an overall favourable teacher's estimate. The results of the maternal interview given in the Appendix show very clearly major class differences in the reported preparation of the child for the current educational experience of the infant school.

We would like to state here as we have written in the main text that our aim is not the criticism of teachers, but rather to raise questions about conditions, contexts and practices which we have the power to change.

Note

1 Recently Ingleby and Cooper (1974) carried out a study of the rating behaviour of infant-school teachers in which the criteria were produced by the teachers *not* by the researchers. In this study, care was taken to obtain criteria that the teachers actually employed. We were agreeably surprised to find that the rating criteria produced by the small sample of teachers was broadly similar to the one we had created.

Introduction Sample, methods and perspectives

The studies which we shall report in this Sociological Research Unit Monograph form a part of a larger group of research enquiries into the relationships between social class, family structures and the use of language, with special reference to education. A description of the full range of our enquiries is given in the Introduction to the first Sociological Research Unit Monograph (Brandis and Henderson, 1970). We shall give here a description of the sample, methods and data relevant to the research reported in this volume.

Sample of children

Two geographically and socially discrete areas in London were selected. One area is in East London and it is overwhelmingly working class in social composition. The second area is in South-east London, and it is overwhelmingly middle class in social composition. It is also an area which has returned a Conservative majority since the war. The correlation between area and social class is 0·74. Social class is measured on a ten-point scale which is based upon the occupation and education of the parents (see Brandis and Henderson, 1970). Thirteen schools were selected from the working-class area and five schools were selected from the middle-class area.

Criteria of selection

Working-class area

The selection of schools in the working-class area was controlled by the requirements of an experimental design created to further the evaluation of an exploratory language programme set up in three schools. Thus schools were selected in this area according to the following criteria:

1 No schools were to have nursery school-feeders.
2 No schools were to be denominational schools.
3 All schools were to have two heads: one infant school and one junior school.
4 All schools were to show a similar distribution of 11+ scores averaged over a three-year period.

On the basis of the above criteria, thirteen schools were selected.[1] The nine schools which formed the experimental design met all four criteria; four schools which were chosen to increase the within-social class differentiation of the sample met all criteria with the exception of the last. The nine schools were grouped into sets of three, and schools were allocated randomly to each set. Group one contained the three schools in which we carried out the exploratory language programme; group two contained three schools where we created a simulated intervention. Here we met the teachers and discussed with them day-by-day problems of teaching, but we did not ourselves draw attention to problems of language use; neither did the teachers emphasise these problems in their discussions (Gahagan and Gahagan, 1970). Group three consisted of three schools which served as a control. No discussions took place with the teachers and the mothers of the children in these schools were given only a short form of the interview (confined to simple demographic information about the family) which we gave to all the mothers of the children.

Middle-class area

We worked very closely with the officers of the LEA and selected five schools whose catchment areas were such that they would yield differentiation within a broad middle-class band.

We studied the children who formed a new two-year intake to the above schools from their first day to the end of their third year. A major requirement of the research was that the children in all the school classes were to be kept together for the three-year period, i.e. no streaming of the children should take place for the life of the research.[2] Every school class contained sample children and non-sample children because of intakes into the class at other periods in the year. *Every teacher of the children knew who were the sample children.*

Table I.1 sets out the total sample.

Data

Mothers of the children were interviewed approximately four months before the sample child went to school for the first time. After the

TABLE I.1 *The total sample*[3]

LEA	*Experimental level*	*No. of schools*	*No. of children*
Group 1	Language intervention	3	83
Group 2	Simulated intervention	3	79
Group 3	Control	3	69
Group 4		4	77
Groups 1–4 Working class		13	308
Group 5 Middle class		5	153
Total		18	461

children had been in school for three weeks, they completed three IQ tests: the Raven's Progressive Matrices (a non-verbal test), the Crichton Scale (a test of active vocabulary) and the English Version of the Peabody Picture Vocabulary Test, EPVT (a test of passive vocabulary). At six years of age, the children in the working-class area completed the full-scale WISC, and the children in the middle-class area completed the short form of this test. We were forced to use the short form for reasons of economy. However, the correlation between the short and full scale version of the WISC in the working-class area is 0·90.

At the end of the children's first year at school, we decided to ask the teachers to rate various aspects of the children's behaviour in the class and also to assess their future school career. We gave the same rating schedule to the different teachers who taught the children for the second school year again at the end of the school year. Table I.2 gives the rating schedule.

TABLE I.2 *Assessment of Children*[4]

In making your assessment, please consider the child in relation to the other children in the class.
Please tick where appropriate

1 *Explanation*
Does the child come up to you on his own accord to explain or tell you about people, things, what he's done, etc.?

Frequently	*Average*	*Rarely*

2 *Questioning*
Does the child come up to you and ask you questions about people, things, class work, etc.?

Frequently	*Average*	*Rarely*

3 *Answering*
Does the child reply to your questioning:

Fluently	*Average*	*With difficulty*

4 How would you assess the child on the following characteristics in comparison with the other children in the class:

	**	*	0	*	**	
Aggressive						Withdrawn
Independent						Dependent
Attentive						Restless
Co-operative						Unco-operative

Legend: ** = very * = a little 0 = average
Example: Aggressive——Withdrawn

In the above table you will see pairs of opposing characteristics. If you think that the child is very aggressive, tick ** on the left-hand side. If you think he is very withdrawn, tick ** on the right-hand side. If you think he is a little aggressive, tick * on the left-hand side. If you think he is a little withdrawn, tick * on the right-hand side. If you think the child shows average behaviour for his class, tick 0.
Use only *one* tick for each pair of characteristics.

5 *Social Behaviour*
What does the child do during free activity or play times:

Play by himself	*Play with others*	*Seek teacher or adult*

6 *Brightness*
Would you say the child is:

Bright	*Average*	*Weak*

7 How well do you think the child will do in his/her school career, taking into account all your knowledge of him/her:

Very well	*Average*	*Not very well*

Sample of teachers

We should like to emphasise that the Sociological Research Unit in *no* way influenced the selection of teachers who taught the sample children. The schools allocated teachers to classrooms in accordance with their normal annual procedures. No teachers were aware (to our knowledge) of the experimental language programme except, of course, the teachers involved. The heads of all schools in the working-class area were told, in confidence, of all details of the research (*except the results of the testing or assessing of the children*) and we have no reason to believe that this confidence was not fully kept. All teachers held qualified teacher status.

Adjustments to the original sample

Children

The number of children in the research reported in this volume is a function of those children who were left in the sample by the end of the second year, and the number for whom we had full IQ data and complete maternal and family data. (See also under Teachers.)

Teachers

In the middle-class area two schools in the first term split their intake in two classes. Streaming was *not* the basis of the division. Thus these two schools simply produced four rating – re-rating systems. In the second year the remaining three schools were forced to split the first-year class into two separate classes at the beginning of the second year. One school class from each of the above schools was excluded from the sample.

Rationale for exclusion of teachers and children

1 In the working-class area two classes had to be excluded because the first- and second-year teacher was the same person.

2 One class was excluded in each area because the children were not exposed to the teacher for a complete year.

3 As a result of the splitting of the sample children into two classes, in the middle-class area, two classes contained very few children; only five in each.

The rationale for exclusion under 1 and 2 is self-evident. In the case of 3 the small numbers in each class are more likely to yield perfect correlations or zero variances. There is also the difficulty of rejecting the null hypothesis when such a test is carried out on small samples.[5]

Thus we were forced to exclude six possible rating and re-rating systems. The final sample is given in Table I.3. The unit of analysis is not a school, but a *school class*. We thus have as the final sample 34 teachers (17 rating and re-rating systems) and 295 children.[6]

TABLE I.3 *The final sample*

Type of classroom	*No. of classrooms*	*No. of children*
Language intervention programme	3	65
Simulated intervention, control and other working-class schools	7	127
Working-class LEA	10	192
Middle-class LEA	7	103
Total	17	295

Exclusion of one question from the rating schedule

We were forced to exclude question five (the question about the child's behaviour during free activity or play time) because 80 per cent of the children were rated as playing with other children. This rating is dominated by a single category. Further, the first-year and second-year ratings appear to be completely unrelated to each other. In other words, the scale suffers not only from an inability to produce an ordering in the response, but empirically it possesses severely reduced variance and a zero stability.

Research perspective

In the reports we shall present, we must emphasise that our focus is upon *teachers*, not children. We have *no* observational records of the children, as a result we do not know the *validity* of the teachers' judgments. We do not know what counts for any one teacher as aggressive, co-operative, independent or attentive behaviour of the child. We do not know what counts as fluent answering; what counts as a question or explanation which achieves a significance in the teachers' memory. Our ratings are ratings of *broad classes* of pupil behaviour. We know something about the *reliability* of the teachers' ratings *within* and between each time period. We are able however to relate the ratings to a range of background variables; family social-class position, an index of maternal communication and control, the sex and measured ability of the child. What we are studying are the *judgments* of the teachers and the implicit model which these judgments may presuppose. We are concerned with differences in this implicit model (which we shall infer from the ratings) held by teachers in the working-class and middle-class areas and we are interested in any change in this model across the two sets of ratings. From another point of view, the ratings give us some idea of what is relevant to the teacher. In as much as this is the case, we are studying the structure of such relevance. It is a fair inference to state that that which is relevant to the teacher eventually shapes the behaviour which the pupil *learns* to offer.

In this way, the criteria of the teacher becomes the criteria which the child takes over to judge his own behaviour and the behaviour of others; but this transfer of criteria is never perfect. How the criteria are transferred, how the child acquires the interpretative principles implicit and explicit in the teachers' behaviour is beyond the scope of this study. The picture which we shall offer is limited by the assumptions of our methods; and *every* method is so limited. All research 'truths' are partial 'truths'. And the truth of research is no more than the meaning of the method.

Our report is divided into two main sections and the second section presupposes the first. We shall therefore briefly discuss the first section. In this section, which inevitably is highly technical, the rationale for the statistical analysis is given in considerable detail. This section is not only important; it is crucial. In as much as its logic is invalid, then the second section is *also* invalid. We clearly believe that, given our present limitations, we have carried out an appropriate statistical description, but this does not mean that, in its own right, it is beyond discussion and criticism. This first section contains a discussion which focuses upon the *similarities* in the ratings between the two areas. Here we discuss what is *common* to the ratings as a whole.

The second section is deliberately non-technical. All that is required of the reader is an understanding of correlations limited to a recognition of differences in their size. We shall give in the text the correlational magnitudes which are statistically significant. We shall also point out what we consider to be interesting trends. In this section we shall be concentrating upon the *differences* between the teachers' ratings in the middle-class and working-class areas and the relation of the background variables to these differences.

The appendix contains a selection from the results of the first interview of the mothers in the sample, which was carried out before the sample child went to school for the first time. We have given here answers to questions which bear upon the preparation of the child for the infant school. The sample of children in the study is the same as the sample of children who were rated by the teachers, with the exception of those children who were in the three control schools in the working-class area.

Finally, we would like to emphasise that we are not concerned to be critical of teachers, for teachers are constrained by events, contexts and conditions which are often *not* of their making. It is too easy for a critic to pontificate from the comfort and security of a concern which rarely takes him into a classroom. The wisdom of such a critic would rarely be relevant for a week, let alone a term, in some of the school classes which society constructs for its teachers.

Notes

1 There were thirty-seven primary schools in this LEA.

2 We had to relax this demand in the middle-class area, as the schools were forced to create additional classes. There was no evidence that these classes were introduced to develop streams.

3 Subsequent statistical analysis showed that there was no difference between the general rating patterns in the four groups of schools in the working-class area.

4 The reader should note that although question 1 and question 2, respectively, are headed 'Explanation' and 'Questioning', which provide a key orientation for the teachers towards a *general class* of verbal activity, the contents of the class do vary. The dimensions we created for the assessment of the perceived characteristics of the children suffers because we do not know what counts for the teachers as exemplars of each characteristic. This is important in the case of the dimensions independent/dependent, attentive/restless, co-operative/unco-operative, as there is likely to be a fair degree of agreement about the referents for those characteristics, but the omission is much more serious for the aggressive/withdrawn dimension. We could have asked the teachers to give examples of the pupil's behaviour which they were asked to scale. We were reluctant to do this, as the teachers, especially in the working-class area, had given up so much of their time to assist the research.

5 Subsequent statistical analysis showed that it was inappropriate to include these school classes in the sample.

6 We carried out an analysis upon the group of children who left the area and we found that the group did not differ in their IQ scores, nor was there any difference between their parents' social-class position, and the social-class position of the parents who remained in the sample.

Part I An enquiry into the structure and origins of teachers' ratings

Walter Brandis

Chapter 1 The approach

Despite widespread pretence to the contrary, a piece of research in the human sciences rarely begins with a body of propositions sufficiently coherent and integrated to be dignified with the label 'theory'. Fortunately, the academic status of our propositional springboard is not at issue, for it never really existed. The rating-questionnaire which is under scrutiny here was initially constructed to obtain supplementary information from teachers about verbal, social and cognitive traits in the sample children, and no specific hypotheses were formulated to guide an analysis of the rating-scores in their own right. It is not intended to make good that omission by trawling for theories in the literature, or by making up a theory from which findings in the research are supposed to have emerged. Accordingly, this study is presented as arising out of the data, and the account begins with a brief review of the data matrix.

The sample and measures originally obtained by the SRU are described in the Introduction at the beginning of this book. It need only be restated that the SRU sample consists of all new intake two-year infants in thirteen primary schools selected from a working-class LEA, and five primary schools selected from a middle-class LEA. Of the working-class LEA schools, nine were specifically recruited into the SRU sample for an experimental design to test the effectiveness of a language intervention programme, the programme itself being implemented in three schools. The mothers of virtually all sample children were interviewed before the children started school, and some or all the children were subjected to a variety of test situations throughout their infant-school career, including a number of IQ tests at the beginning of each school year. At the end of each school year, every infant-school teacher was asked to complete a standard rating-questionnaire[1] for all sample children in her class. By way of introduction to any study of ratings, the structure and content of such a questionnaire requires some comment.

The teachers' rating-questionnaire

The rating-questionnaire submitted to each teacher at the end of the first and second years is set out in the Introduction. Its constituent rating-questions may be described in terms both of their formal design, and of their meaning-content. The meaning-content can, in turn, be split into a descriptive and a prescriptive component. On a descriptive level, the concern of the SRU with the verbal behaviour of infant-school children is reflected in the formulation of three rating-questions, located at the beginning of the questionnaire, to deal specifically with the quantity and quality of children's speech in the classroom situation. 'Explanation' and 'Questioning' ask for a description of the frequency with which the child makes verbal approaches to the teacher, while 'Answering' asks for an evaluation of the fluency with which the child responds to verbal interactions initiated by the teacher. The four rating-dimensions which follow are much more general in scope, in that they ask for overall estimates of classroom behaviour rather than evaluations limited to specific behavioural areas. They split into two clearly separate pairs, with 'Aggressiveness' and 'Independence' focusing on the active autonomy of the child, and 'Attentiveness' and 'Co-operativeness' on the submission of the child to the teacher-centred order of the classroom. Of the last three rating-questions, 'Social behaviour' asks for a straight description of the child's social attachments outside the formal classroom system. Finally, 'Brightness' and 'Future school career' are academically-oriented rating-questions, the former asking the teacher to evaluate the child's intellectual capacity and the latter his academic potential. 'Future school career' differs from the remainder of the rating-questionnaire in that it is a prediction, whereas all the other rating-questions are asking for a description or evaluation of existing behaviours and dispositions.

It seems a general characteristic of rating-questionnaires that they are value-loaded, that one response may be seen as generally preferential to another in any particular rating-question. The SRU rating-questionnaire is no exception. Thus, for a child to do 'Very well' in his school career is socially and educationally preferable to his doing 'Not very well', and similarly with 'Bright' to 'Weak', 'Co-operative' to 'Unco-operative', 'Attentive' to 'Restless', 'Independent' to 'Dependent', and answering 'Fluently' to answering 'With difficulty'. These rating-categories are self-evidently prescriptive as well as descriptive in character. Categories describing frequency, on the other hand, are prescriptively neutral, but the verbal approach of child to teacher is almost certainly a valued activity in the modal infant classroom, so for a child to ask teacher questions 'Often' is likely to be preferred to his asking them 'Rarely', and the same preference is likely in the case of a child explaining things to teacher. This leaves only two other rating-questions without obvious value-bias: 'Social behaviour', which is again purely descriptive, and the 'Aggressive-Withdrawn' opposition, where, if anything, both categories seem to have an equally undesirable connotation.

On a formal level, the first three and the last three rating-questions were each designed as a matrix of *n* children by three categories. The middle four rating-dimensions, however, were bracketed together in a 'semantic differential' design, in this case a matrix of four ratings by five categories for each of *n* children. Three basic differences between the two designs may be noted: (i) the first presents a column of children for each rating, the second a column of ratings for each child; (ii) the first requires the teacher to choose from three categories, the second from five categories; (iii) the first names a dimension, clarifies its meaning in a supporting text, and names each category, whereas the second merely states two polar categories and leaves the respondent to impose his own interpretation on the space between.

An orientation to the study of teachers' ratings

It should be emphasised that the terms of reference which guided the selection of the sample and gathering of data did not explicitly include a projected study of teachers' ratings. But having been obtained, these ratings may be focused in an interesting way. Any device for measuring is intended to give information about the things measured, but it can also be used as information about the people who make the measures, or who do the measuring. Those who believe in the infallibility of professionals will see a teacher's rating in the same way as a doctor's diagnosis, a judge's summing-up or a referee's decision: it gives information about the thing being rated, diagnosed, summed-up or decided upon. Such a view is consistent only with a sociology that is completely servile to the society in which it is located. To reject it is to allow teachers' ratings to be used as information not about the children, but about the teachers.

Despite an absence of any direct information about teachers in the SRU sample (except that all are female and qualified), it is the teachers, not the children, who will be the basic units of study. The study will begin by describing the one-year stability of each terminal rating across teachers, as a kind of practical analogue to reliability. It will then consider the internal structure of the rating-set, and continue by examining how far set and individual ratings relate to attributes which the child brings to school. The analysis is therefore focused on teachers' responses to the rating-questionnaire such that its scope broadens at each stage; any rating is examined first by reference to a repetition of itself, then by reference to other rating-questions, and, finally, by reference to variables external to the rating-set. In the concluding section, the relationship between IQ and teachers' ratings will receive special attention, and a number of comments on measurement and the social structure will emerge.

Adjustments to the data matrix

In most of the classrooms which constitute the SRU sample, one teacher was in charge for the first year, and a different teacher was in charge for the second year. As a minimally standardising tactic, any classroom in which the first- and second-year teachers were the same person, or in which the sample children had not been exposed to the rating-teacher for the whole school year, is rejected from the teachers' ratings sample, and so, for other technical reasons, are classrooms which contain very few sample children. The sample that remains consists of 34 teachers in 17 classrooms, with repeated ratings obtained for a total of 295 children.

Throughout the study, these classrooms will be grouped by whether they are located in the middle-class or the working-class LEA, and if the latter, whether they have been tampered with by the SRU to adjust their teaching styles to a language intervention programme.[2] At each stage of the analysis, some attempt will be made to assess the degree to which (i) the ratings of individual teachers may be construed as random samples from a rating-procedure characteristic of the group, and (ii) the mean ratings of groups of teachers may be construed as random samples from a generalised rating-procedure.

All the ratings will be used in the analysis with the exception of 'Social behaviour', which is excluded on the grounds that its scale consists of unordered nominal categories. The remaining nine rating-questions each consist of scale categories that are symmetrically ordered around a notional average, and may be described as ordinal-approaching-interval in measurement level. In order to make the powerful apparatus of parametric statistics available – not because it is then easier to attain any desired significance level, but because the scope for statistical control and exploration becomes so much greater – simple interval scaling is assumed for every rating-question.

Notes

1 The rating-questionnaire was invented by Mrs J. Jones and Professor B. Bernstein.
2 Strictly speaking, the simulated intervention schools should also be classified as a separate group. However, the content of discussions with researchers was determined by what the teachers in this group thought to be educationally important, and language received no special emphasis. The simulated intervention can be seen as merely heightening the teachers' initial definition of the situation, rather than altering that definition as is implied by the language intervention programme. On a practical level, one of the schools from this group has been rejected from the teachers' ratings sample, and throughout the analysis differences between the two remaining schools are usually considerably larger than differences between those schools combined and the other non-programme schools in the working-class LEA.

Chapter 2 Stability of teachers' ratings

A rating is an evaluation of things or persons by a judge in terms of a stated characteristic. When a judge rates a group of subjects, the rating is used to locate the relative position of persons on a dimension, and in that sense it is an alternative measurement procedure to testing. However, testing generates scores on a fairly rigorous inferential basis (allegedly), whereas a set of ratings is no more than the general opinion of a judge. Even when a rating-question is standardised so that it can be submitted in identical form to each of any number of potential judges, several possible sources of between-judge variation remain. These may be identified as (i) understanding the rating-question; (ii) having provided opportunities for subjects to display the understood trait; (iii) having observed the trait-displays; (iv) recalling those observations in response to the rating-question; and (v) allocating that recall to discrete rating categories. Within the framework set by the variably understood rating-question, each judge in effect constitutes a unique combination of experimental, observational and scoring procedures, with variable time-lapse between experiment and observation on the one hand and scoring on the other.

More precisely, a rating-score may be theoretically partitioned, like a test-score, into common and unique components, and the unique component may be further partitioned into specific and error components. The common component can be defined as the hypothetical mean rating of the total population of judges over a total population of rating-circumstances. The specific component is the additional rating-score necessary to produce the hypothetical mean rating of the total population of rating-circumstances for a particular judge, and so may be interpreted as the unique bias of that judge. The external constraints which bound the population of rating-circumstances should be contained in the definition of the population of judges. Finally, the difference between the common plus specific score and the observed score is the error component, which may, in part at least, be interpreted as a function of the judge's indifference to the rating process for the dimension being rated.

A set of simultaneous ratings by different judges from an appropriately defined population gives an estimate of the common component of observed rating scores. If the ratings are not simultaneous, then there is an additional specific component which has nothing to do with the unique bias of a particular judge: trait-change in the subjects being rated. This could be defined by reference to some 'real' trait, whatever that may be, but a lot of difficulties are avoided by defining it as the change in the common component. In short, trait-change is what would be seen to be a trait-change by all possible judges. A rating-rerating stability coefficient across judges, then, is the component of the rating-question common to those judges, minus the perceived trait-change over the rating-rerating time interval.

There is another aspect of reliability theory which requires special attention in this context, and that is variation between judges in the consistency of a rating-question. In terms of either a hypothetical covariance matrix of simultaneous ratings, or an observed covariance matrix of stabilities, the amount of rating-variance which is common will vary between judges. This notion is conveniently summarised by the word 'transferability', defined by Cattell (1964) as 'the degree to which a test retains its properties across an agreed standard range of reference populations'.[1] This definition has a high level of generality, and no injustice is done to its formal elements if 'test' is understood to denote a rating-question, and 'an agreed standard range of reference populations' is understood to denote a population of potential judges. When these substitutions are focused on the common component of any rating-question, reference can be made to the transferability of a rating-question across judges, with the proviso that the consideration of stabilities will necessarily involve a confounding between non-transferability and differential trait-change.

The mean stability

At the beginning of the rating-questionnaire, teachers were asked to rate the children in their class by reference to a classroom average, so any differences between teachers' mean ratings should be quite arbitrary.[2] In order to exclude these differences from an overall stability coefficient, a description of rating-stability can be made for each classroom, and these descriptions pooled into a general statement, which may be viewed as a weighted mean. The variation between classrooms about that mean can then be calculated and compared with the variation expected on the basis of conventional random sampling.

There are two different routes by which a pooled stability coefficient may be obtained, and they lead to different answers. In one, stability is described by the covariance matrix from which it was initially calculated, and, in the other, it is transformed into a z-value by Fisher's r to z transformation. The pooling of covariance matrices tacitly assumes that differences in rating-variance are meaningful, that these differences represent different heterogeneities within classrooms rather than arbitrarily different scoring conventions of teachers. The pooling of z-values obviously ignores any weighting by variance, and it assigns a relatively greater weight both to larger correlations and to larger groups of subjects. Table 2.1 shows the stability of each rating-question in the total sample, obtained first by pooling covariance matrices and then by pooling z-values.

TABLE 2.1 *Pooled classroom stability coefficients obtained by two different routes for each of nine rating-questions in the total sample*

	r *(covariance matrices)*	r *(z-values)*
Explanation	0·436	0·462
Questioning	0·354	0·353
Answering	0·565	0·587
Aggressiveness	0·471	0·541
Independence	0·496	0·506
Attentiveness	0·492	0·605
Co-operativeness	0·428	0·515
Brightness	0·705	0·723
Future school career	0·658	0·661

Predictably, the pooled z-values tend to give higher estimates of stability than the pooled covariance matrices. However, the ordering of rating-questions in terms of stability is roughly the same by both methods. Teachers' rating of 'Brightness' is the most stable (0·70 via pooled covariance matrices, 0·72 via pooled z-values), followed by 'Future school career' (0·66, 0·66). At the other end, 'Questioning' is the least stable (0·35, 0·35), followed by 'Explanation' (0·44, 0·46) and 'Co-operativeness' (0·43, 0·52). In general, the rating-questions have a stability of around 0·50, with the academically-oriented items being considerably more stable, and the quantity of speech items somewhat less stable.

Anticipating the discussion on the measurement of variation

around these mean stability coefficients, a brief glance may be given to the three groups of classrooms which constitute the total sample. There are, in fact, no significant differences between the middle-class and working-class LEAs for any stability coefficient through either method. Within the working-class LEAs, there are again no significant differences between language programme schools and the remainder, with one important exception: the *z*-value for 'Answering' is significantly higher in the language programme schools ($p < 0{\cdot}02$). Indeed, 'Answering' has a higher stability in the language programme schools (0·72, 0·75) than have either 'Brightness' (0·66, 0·69) or 'Future school career' (0·69, 0·69).[3]

What inferences can be made from these differential stabilities? Trait-change cannot be separated from the component unique to teachers, nor can the uniqueness due to bias be separated from that due to indifference. However, variations in the stability of 'Answering' do provide a useful clue about high stability. It seems unlikely that the language programme has actually reduced relative change among children in the quality of speech. The significantly higher stability of 'Answering' in the language programme schools must then be a consequence of a larger common component, and this would be a function both of the homogenising influence of the programme in terms of what constitutes fluent answering to the teachers, and of the greater attention paid to the quality of speech as a consequence of that programme. The stability of 'Brightness' and 'Future school career' throughout the total sample is much the same as that of 'Answering' in the language programme schools. Given constancy of trait-change between the dimensions rated, it could be argued that what the SRU did to the language programme teachers in terms of 'Answering', the social and educational system as a whole has done to all infant-school teachers in terms of 'Brightness' and 'Future school career'. If that is so, then academic criteria occupy a place of special prominence in the perceptual apparatus of infant-school teachers.

Variation between classrooms

The variations of classroom covariance matrices and *z*-values around their respective means may be indicated via a comparison with the variations expected on a conventional random sampling basis. The homogeneity of covariance matrices can be assessed by using an approximate χ^2-test devised by Box (1950) and recommended by Winer (1962),[4] while an exact χ^2-test can be used to assess the homogeneity of *z*-values.[5] A χ^2 is simply an observed sum-of-squares divided by a (theoretical) population variance, and so, allowing for degrees of freedom, may be viewed as a controlled variance of the classrooms around the sample mean. Table 2.2 shows both sets of χ^2-values for each rating-question over the total sample.

TABLE 2.2 *Approximate χ^2-values indicating the heterogeneity between covariance matrices and exact χ^2-values indicating the heterogeneity between classroom z-values for each of nine rating-questions over the total sample*

	χ^2 *(covariance matrices)* $df = 48$	χ^2 *(z-values)* $df = 16$
Explanation	36·54	16·36
Questioning	66·57, $p < 0{\cdot}05$	26·53, $p < 0{\cdot}05$
Answering	77·18, $p < 0{\cdot}01$	25·88
Aggressiveness	140·05, $p < 0{\cdot}001$	38·73, $p < 0{\cdot}01$
Independence	120·85, $p < 0{\cdot}001$	29·68, $p < 0{\cdot}05$
Attentiveness	143·90, $p < 0{\cdot}001$	38 95, $p < 0{\cdot}01$
Co-operativeness	134·48, $p < 0{\cdot}001$	19·52
Brightness	55·58	17·08
Future school career	59·37	9·57

Taking the usual significance levels, the null hypothesis of matrix-homogeneity is rejected for no less than six of the nine rating-questions; that of z-homogeneity is rejected for only four rating-questions, and at much less extreme probability levels. On the whole, then, covariance matrices, and to a lesser extent z-values, tend to vary more between classrooms than would be expected on a conventional random sampling basis. However, to compare the variabilities of covariance matrices with those of z-values by significance levels is a little misleading, because the larger the degrees of freedom, the smaller a ratio need be to attain any desired level of significance. In this situation, a proper comparison of variabilities should ignore significance levels, and instead make use of a controlled variance estimate, which is best achieved here by taking the ratio of each χ^2-value to its degrees of freedom. It then turns out that z-values vary more than covariance matrices for the three speech items at the beginning of the rating-questionnaire, but covariance matrices vary more than z-values for the remaining six rating-questions.

However, a closer look at the relative variations of the speech ratings does reveal an interesting trend. The χ^2 for covariance matrices, the difference between this χ^2 and χ^2 for z-values, and, for that matter, the ratio of the first to the second χ^2, all show a clear increase for successive rating-questions from 'Explanation' to 'Answering'. There is also an increase in the variability of z-values from 'Explanation' to 'Questioning', but there is no further increase to 'Answering'. Moreover, while the variability of z-values for 'Explanation' is low, it is not the lowest in the rating-questionnaire, whereas the variability of covariance matrices for 'Explanation' is. All the evidence, in fact, points to a steady increase in the variability of rating-variances from the beginning of the rating-questionnaire. Or to put it another way, the variability of variances is depressed at the beginning of the rating-questionnaire, and blossoms out as the questionnaire proceeds. Since the injunction to rate 'the child in relation to other children in the class' occurs before 'Explanation', but not before 'Questioning' or 'Answering', it is reasonable to suppose that judges take care to distribute their responses fairly evenly at the beginning of the rating-questionnaire, but idiosyncratic styles of response distribution emerge as the questionnaire proceeds. If this supposition is correct, the quite unusual lack of matrix-heterogeneity for 'Explanation' is simply a function of its arbitrary position at the beginning of the rating-questionnaire.

Despite a hypothesised depression at the beginning of the rating-questionnaire, the variation of covariance matrices is generally greater than that of z-values and, when this is combined with substantially larger degrees of freedom, matrix-homogeneity becomes the exception rather than the rule. But there are degrees of heterogeneity. Even a cursory examination of Table 2.2 reveals that matrix-heterogeneity is especially powerful in each of the four rating-questions which are bracketed together in the semantic differential design. z-values also tend to be more heterogeneous among these rating-questions but by no means as emphatically as covariance matrices. Once again, then, it seems that rating-variances are the chief culprit. And the explanation this time would seem to lie in the form of the questions, that each of the ways in which the semantic differential differs from the conventional design induces greater inconsistency in the distribution of responses between judges. The immediate referent for scoring is now not other subjects but other ratings, and the discipline of three named categories within a clearly explicated dimension is replaced by the licence of five unnamed categories on a dimension identified by only two words.

So the property of a rating-question which appears to be the most variable is its variance, and there are plausible grounds for arguing that this variation reflects idiosyncratic scoring procedures on the part of the teachers rather than variations in trait-variance. Expressed in another way, the rating-property which is least transferable between infant-school teachers is rating-variance, with the qualification that its transferability is strongly influenced both by the proximity of the rating-question to the front of the questionnaire, and by the form in which the rating-question is put to the teachers. Since the status of observed rating-variance is so clearly suspect, every rating-variance is set to unity for each teacher in the analyses that follow.

Apart from 'Explanation', there are two rating-questions for which the null hypothesis of matrix-homogeneity is not rejected, and which demonstrate a very high order of z-homogeneity: 'Brightness' and 'Future school career'. These are also the two most stable rating-questions. In other words, teachers appear to be able to produce standard ratings for these two questions in a way that they are unable to do with other rating-questions. 'Brightness' and 'Future school career' are not only the most stable judgments made across teachers within classrooms, they also receive the most consistent usage between classrooms. It seems that infant-school teachers are at their least idiosyncratic, and at their most culturally coherent, when making judgments about the present intellectual and future academic life of the infant-school child. It may be concluded that even in the infant school, when the child is only five or six years old, teachers as a group achieve more consensus on the child's intelligence and academic potential than on any other aspect of his make-up.

Notes

1 Cattell actually suggests two varieties of transferability. The first he describes as 'constancy of validity', and the second as 'some higher order derivative simultaneously giving weight to constancy in all test properties, viz: validity, reliability, homogeneity, standardisation, etc'. Whichever is used, Cattell's intent is constancy of the measure (test or rating) across different populations of those who are measured, whereas it has been adapted here to refer to constancy of the measure (rating-question) across those who do the measuring.

2 The stabilities of between-classroom rating are, in fact, always much lower than those of within-classroom ratings. This emphasises at least the relative arbitrariness of mean ratings, and provides empirical justification for the exclusion of between-group statistics.

3 It should be noted that the stability of 'Answering' for the rest of the working-class LEA does not differ significantly from that for the middle-class LEA. The stability for the total sample, excluding the language programme schools, reduces to 0·51 (via covariance matrices) and 0·52 (via z-values).

4 The description of Box's test in our edition of Winer contains errors in both formula (p.370) and example (p.373). It is the writer's experience that errors appear in other parts of this edition.

5 This test is described in Edwards (p.83). The χ^2-value is simply the sum-of-squares of the z-values.

Chapter 3 Structure of the rating-set

The description of rating-consistency between times/teachers may be viewed as a preliminary, quasi-psychometric, characterisation of individual rating-questions. It is interesting, though, how even at that austere level, a pattern emerges which suggests distinct contours in the topography of teacher-culture at infant-school level. The next stage, which is to trace the manner in which a teacher's responses to different rating-questions relate to each other, should generate much firmer inferences in this direction.

Without prejudicing the shape of subsequent analysis, an introductory overview of the rating-set would be useful. In order to get a general idea of the relational patterns which emerge from the rating-questionnaire, Table 3.1 shows the pooled correlations between the sum of first- and second-year ratings in the total sample.

TABLE 3.1 *Pooled correlations between the sum of first- and second-year ratings for the total sample*

	Exp.	*Ques.*	*Ans.*	*Agg.*	*Ind.*	*Att.*	*Coop.*	*Bri.*	*Fsc.*
Explanation	1·000								
Questioning	0·764	1·000							
Answering	0·610	0·670	1·000						
Aggressiveness	0·502	0·448	0·379	1·000					
Independence	0·397	0·416	0·584	0·459	1·000				
Attentiveness	0·221	0·344	0·508	−0·094	0·402	1·000			
Co-operativeness	0·300	0·392	0·470	−0·122	0·346	0·778	1·000		
Brightness	0·370	0·532	0·734	0·190	0·595	0·680	0·562	1·000	
Future school career	0·363	0·503	0·730	0·131	0·548	0·714	0·591	0·909	1·000

These correlations are almost invariably positive and usually high, with only one rating, 'Aggressiveness', having pretensions to occasional orthogonality. But there are several clusters in the matrix.

'Brightness' and 'Future school career' are so highly correlated that they must be considered virtually indistinguishable. Two other powerful, though weakly interrelated, clusters are 'Explanation' – 'Questioning' and 'Attentiveness' – 'Co-operativeness'. Any pair of ratings in the set is likely to be highly correlated, but, taken as a whole, the rating-set is definitely lumpy in character.

For the sake of balance, Table 3.2 shows the pooled correlations between the difference of first- and second-year ratings.

TABLE 3.2 *Pooled correlations between the difference of first- and second-year ratings for the total sample*

	Exp.	*Ques.*	*Ans.*	*Agg.*	*Ind.*	*Att.*	*Coop.*	*Bri.*	*Fsc.*
Explanation	1·000								
Questioning	0·502	1·000							
Answering	0·264	0·248	1·000						
Aggressiveness	0·153	0·183	0·135	1·000					
Independence	0·116	0·104	0·137	0·217	1·000				
Attentiveness	0·181	0·188	0·227	−0·050	0·046	1·000			
Co-operativeness	0·249	0·313	0·263	0·029	0·058	0·523	1·000		
Brightness	0·190	0·178	0·252	0·182	0·144	0·178	0·175	1·000	
Future school career	0·054	0·151	0·261	0·096	0·082	0·202	0·251	0·542	1·000

These rating difference-scores are simply the time/teacher-specific ratings, and one important component in the correlations between them is response-set. It is not surprising, then, that nearly every correlation in the matrix is positive, most of them falling between 0·10 and 0·30. Once again, however, there are clusters. In this case, the ratings separate out into four distinct pairs: 'Explanation' – 'Questioning', 'Attentiveness' – 'Co-operativeness', 'Brightness' – 'Future school career', and, to a lesser extent, 'Aggressiveness' – 'Independence'. Only 'Answering' appears to have avoided this clustering pattern. Each cluster consists of two contiguous ratings, and given the substantive meaning-content common to each pair, it is evident that there are powerful local response-sets to the rating-questionnaire.

Halo effect and general factor

Despite its correlational variability, Table 3.1 does illustrate a general feature noted in all studies of teachers' ratings: that ratings tend to be highly correlated; more highly, it is thought, than they would have been had the traits concerned been measured by other means. Different ratings made by the same teacher appear to share a common component over and above that induced by the correlations between the 'real' traits or behaviours of those being rated. In so far as rating-questions are formulated in terms of pro and con categories, this additional common component may be interpreted as a generalised value-judgment. So if a child is highly valued by the teacher, no matter what criteria initially determined the teacher's valuation, that child will tend to be more highly rated in terms of such socially desirable characteristics as ability, motivation, attentiveness, industry, neatness, fluency, creativity and so on.

The common component in a set of ratings derived from a questionnaire like the one in this study may therefore be viewed as a mixture of description and value-judgment. The value-judgment part has been termed 'halo effect', and is a constant irritation to psychometricians who wish to use teachers' ratings as measures of children. But it is very useful to anyone who is interested in teachers. Since the halo effect is part of the rating-set's common component, identification of that component might throw up valuable clues about the major criteria by which a teacher's valuation of children is arrived at.

On a more practical level, when there is a sizeable component common to each of the ratings derived from a rating-questionnaire, the listing of relationships between any variable external to the rating-set and successive ratings would involve, in part, a persistent repetition of the relation between that variable and the common component in the teacher's ratings. Once the common component has been identified it can be partialled out, and the relationship between external variable and ratings independent of the total rating-set (but not necessarily independent of a rating subset) may be ascertained.

In a generally value-loaded rating-questionnaire, the common component induced by a generalised value-judgment is likely to be a critical influence in the production of a 'general factor'. A factor is a hypothesised variable which is derived from, and is intended to account for, the relationships between a set of items. Once a factor has been extracted from a relational matrix, it is identified by reference to the differential correlations of the factor with the items. When the correlation matrix describing a set of items consists predominantly of positive correlations, the first factor will tend to correlate positively with all the items in the set. In so far as the first factor both accounts for a high proportion of variance in each item, and, by the same token, is identified by reference to all the items, it is called a 'general' factor. This is precisely what may be expected from a set of teachers' ratings.

The number of different possible factor solutions to a correlation matrix is theoretically infinite. It has, however, become increasingly fashionable to opt for the principal component method, more particularly since the awesome calculations involved have been routinised into standard computer programs. The special appeal of principal components is that each successive factor accounts for the largest possible proportion of set-variance. The first principal component is therefore the largest possible factor which may be extracted from a virgin correlation matrix. To obtain what, in effect, constitutes a maximally comprehensive description of the rating-set in one go is an attractive proposition, particularly since the primary objective in factoring the rating-set is to obtain a factor with the greatest generality possible. Accordingly, the convention of extracting principal components will not be disturbed here.

Two major problems remain after the appropriate method of factoring has been decided. The first is when to stop factoring, which in this instance has been solved by declaring an interest in the first factor only. The second is sampling. It is assumed that the items being factored have been sampled from one or more populations of items, but there is some mystery about the status of the subjects measured by the item set. In general, the variability of factors across random samples of subjects is not known, so if there are two or more samples of subjects, and the same set of items for each is factored separetely, the variation between the resultant factor patterns cannot be compared with the variation expected on the basis of conventional random sampling.

One classic way of not avoiding this dilemma has been to assign schools/teachers to predetermined groups, factor their pooled ratings, and describe whatever between-group differences in factor patterns catch the eye. It is ironic that the mathematical complexity of modern factor analysis should eventually dissolve into nothing more than a list of descriptive comparisons. Each teacher could, of course, be factored separately, but the increasing volatility of successive factors can make it very difficult, even after rotation, to match factors across teachers. This difficulty is avoided in an analysis concerned only with the general factor since, by definition, matching follows automatically from arranging the vectors in a teacher-item matrix of factor loadings such that the sum of weighted elements in every marginal is positive. Factoring each teacher's ratings separately appears to be a perfectly feasible proposition so long as the research ambition is limited to a general factor. And it is desirable because it produces a non-intuitive criterion, the between-teacher variation, for determining the significance of differences between groups of teachers. It should be added that any attempt to predict first rating-factor scores from characteristics which children bring to school also implies, for the same sort of reasons, that each teacher should be factored separately.

The first principal component

There are thirty-four teachers in the SRU stability sample, so thirty-four factor analyses have been carried out.[1] The first principal component for each teacher is shown in Tables 3.3 (i) and 3.3 (ii).

A cautionary note must accompany these tables. If the nine items in the correlation matrix split into two uncorrelated clusters, then the first principal component will simply be the larger cluster. To describe this factor as 'general' is misleading, in that there is no proper general factor, only two particular ones. The first principal component is, by definition, the largest possible factor in the matrix; it accounts for more of the rating-set than any other factor. But what it accounts for may not be as important to the teacher as the smaller second factor. In a few instances, then, it could be that the valuation implied in the first factor is of only marginal importance to the teacher, and that the second factor contains the critical elements in the teacher's value-orientation. A weakness of this study (and most other studies) is the total lack of evidence to show if and when the largest factor is not the one with the greatest substantive importance. But in a rating-questionnaire which is suffused with value-judgments, a factor other than the first is not likely to achieve this status very often. It is just that a little caution should be exercised when reading lists of first factors such as shown in Tables 3.3 (i) and 3.3 (ii).[2]

The possibility that an occasional first factor does not properly represent the general value-orientation of the teacher must, of course, modify any conclusion drawn from an average of those factors. For example, if consistently differential rating-values are not efficiently absorbed by first factors, pooling the factors could result in a flattening of those differentials. As long as there are no persistent unidirectional biases, however, a summary of first factors across the seventeen classrooms should indicate the differential contributions of individual rating-questions to the teachers' general value-orientation with fair accuracy. Table 3.4 shows the proportion of rating-variance

TABLE 3.3 (i) *The first principal component for each first-year teacher*

School (class)	Factor-item correlations = factor loadings									
	Exp.	*Ques.*	*Ans.*	*Agg.*	*Ind.*	*Att.*	*Co-op.*	*Bri.*	FSC	*Latent root*
Language programme										
11	0·820	0·630	0·764	0·702	0·861	0·455	0·574	0·720	0·756	4·514
12	0·549	0·658	0·812	0·248	0·507	0·819	0·851	0·802	0·829	4·436
13	0·305	0·486	0·811	0·028	0·409	0·728	0·755	0·805	0·899	3·712
Other working class										
22	0·364	0·730	0·917	0·657	0·913	0·878	0·264	0·933	0·927	5·340
23	0·799	0·909	0·895	−0·105	0·497	0·771	0·785	0·813	0·807	5·047
31	0·218	0·440	0·518	−0·067	0·532	0·781	0·909	0·878	0·835	3·702
32	0·845	0·922	0·696	0·850	−0·029	−0·497	−0·471	0·571	0·353	3·690
33	0·801	0·862	0·944	0·728	0·514	0·238	0·138	0·926	0·893	4·800
43	0·275	0·231	0·092	−0·702	−0·807	0·825	0·636	0·674	0·725	3·345
44	0·528	0·096	0·848	0·056	0·889	0·928	0·889	0·860	0·840	4·897
Middle class										
51 (A)	0·821	0·867	0·704	0·763	0·948	0·691	0·771	0·906	0·718	5·811
51 (B)	0·793	0·554	0·750	0·842	0·718	0·247	0·355	0·717	0·750	3·985
52 (A)	0·884	0·829	0·963	0·668	0·905	0·818	0·660	0·946	0·884	6·445
52 (B)	−0·345	−0·236	0·436	0·749	0·900	0·231	0·017	0·925	0·925	3·500
53	0·872	0·778	0·875	0·758	0·767	0·754	0·940	0·705	0·729	5·779
54	0·688	0·763	0·293	0·313	0·415	0·761	0·917	0·760	0·780	4·019
55	0·911	0·862	0·901	0·164	−0·313	0·955	0·899	0·914	0·923	5·914

TABLE 3.3 (ii) *The first principal component for each second-year teacher*

School (class)	Factor-item correlations = factor loadings									Latent root
	Exp.	*Ques.*	*Ans.*	*Agg.*	*Ind.*	*Att.*	*Co-op.*	*Bri.*	FSC	
Language programme										
11	0·865	0·840	0·866	0·263	0·853	0·863	0·873	0·955	0·837	6·119
12	0·812	0·823	0·890	0·259	0·781	0·804	0·817	0·898	0·898	5·731
13	0·436	0·791	0·875	0·449	0·798	0·491	0·760	0·802	0·744	4·435
Other working class										
22	0·648	0·744	0·891	0·336	0·355	0·902	0·689	0·902	0·901	4·920
23	0·727	0·834	0·892	−0·016	0·770	0·720	0·899	0·897	0·923	5·595
31	0·809	0·868	0·837	0·564	0·775	0·774	0·816	0·897	0·897	5·902
32	0·892	0·783	0·748	0·832	0·868	−0·355	−0·092	0·367	0·322	3·787
33	0·041	−0·580	0·512	−0·142	0·533	0·742	0·671	0·785	0·874	3·286
43	0·292	0·922	0·949	−0·895	−0·343	0·930	0·829	0·809	0·900	5·791
44	0·561	0·563	0·715	0·092	0·872	0·813	0·791	0·825	0·744	4·432
Middle class										
51 (A)	0·339	0·839	0·810	−0·195	0·954	0·712	0·825	0·938	0·943	5·377
51 (B)	0·512	0·735	0·581	0·408	0·461	0·757	0·195	0·922	0·922	3·829
52 (A)	0·453	0·835	0·785	0·789	0·922	0·726	−0·096	0·813	0·813	4·850
52 (B)	0·274	0·431	0·947	0·041	0·493	0·879	0·784	0·952	0·952	4·603
53	0·181	0·603	0·798	0·233	0·647	0·789	0·853	0·807	0·807	4·158
54	0·166	0·750	0·833	0·448	0·666	0·829	0·909	0·755	0·841	4·720
55	0·939	0·820	0·887	0·756	0·823	−0·004	0·074	0·838	0·712	4·804

TABLE 3.4 *Proportion of rating-variance accounted for in the total sample by all first and second factors (principal components)*

	First school year			*Second school year*		
	Factor 1	*Factor* 2	*Both factors*	*Factor* 1	*Factor* 2	*Both factors*
Explanation	0·463	0·293	0·756	0·371	0·333	0·704
Questioning	0·485	0·219	0·704	0·589	0·125	0·714
Answering	0·610	0·157	0·767	0·670	0·076	0·746
Aggressiveness	0·330	0·350	0·680	0·208	0·548	0·756
Independence	0·476	0·152	0·628	0·530	0·142	0·672
Attentiveness	0·500	0·246	0·746	0·556	0·218	0·774
Co-operativeness	0·474	0·295	0·769	0·519	0·211	0·730
Brightness	0·684	0·093	0·777	0·725	0·093	0·818
Future school career	*0·666*	*0·091*	*0·757*	*0·712*	*0·108*	*0·820*
Sum	*4·688*	*1·896*	*6·584*	*4·880*	*1·854*	*6·734*
Mean	0·521	0·211	0·732	0·542	0·206	0·748

in the total sample explained by all first factors, and, for comparison, the proportion explained by all second factors. Table 3.5 shows the variation of first factor loadings across teachers for each rating-question. It should be noted that differences between groups of teachers may be attributed entirely to between-teacher fluctuations, so only total sample statistics are given.

TABLE 3.5 *Variation (sums of squares=SS) between all sample teachers in the regression of each rating on first factors, plus F-values and associated significance levels*

	First school year		*Second school year*	
	SS	$F_{16,249}$	*SS*	$F_{16,249}$
Explanation	23·8	2·59‡	20·6	1·92*
Questioning	20·9	2·37†	40·0	5·70‡
Answering	12·6	1·89*	3·9	<1·00
Aggressiveness	46·3	4·05‡	40·6	3·00‡
Independence	52·4	5·85‡	21·8	2·72‡
Attentiveness	29·9	3·50‡	24·7	3·26‡
Co-operativeness	34·3	3·82‡	27·7	3·37‡
Brightness	2·8	<1·00	3·8	<1·00
Future school career	4·0	<1·00	4·6	<1·00

* $= p<0{\cdot}05$, † $= p<0{\cdot}01$, ‡ $= p<0{\cdot}001$

It is evident from Table 3.4 that the first factors dominate the teachers' ratings, for they explain more than half the total rating-variance, whereas the second factors account for only one-fifth. On this level, the first factor clearly averages out as a 'general' factor, and the way it dwarfs the second factor effectively wipes out any claim of the latter to represent teachers' general value-orientation in a generally value-loaded rating-questionnaire. One rating, 'Aggressiveness', is more powerfully associated with the second than the first factors, but 'Aggressiveness' is the only rating left in the set which may be deemed entirely value-neutral. On average, then, the first factor is the overwhelmingly value-laden factor.

The ratings with the highest proportion of variances explained by the first factors – and the lowest proportion explained by the second factors – are 'Brightness', 'Future school career', and, to a lesser extent, 'Answering'. So the first factors, the ones which contain so much value-judgment, are bound up closest of all with the academically-oriented items, and then with quality of speech. Moreover, Table 3.5 shows that, in both school years, the variation across teachers of factor loadings for 'Brightness' and 'Future school career' are no more than would be expected from regression coefficients in a set of random samples, and this is also true for 'Answering' in the second year. All the other variations represent significant departures from the random sampling model. The academically-oriented items and, to a lesser extent, quality of speech are the ratings most closely identified with the first factor, and they are also the ratings whose relationship with that factor is the most consistent across teachers.

Before elaborating a little further on the factor-rating relationships, it is instructive to look at the stability of factors. Table 3.6 shows the first-factor stability, the second-factor stability, and the first-second factor correlations between first- and second-year teachers for each classroom.

The sign attached to correlations involving a second factor need not be treated too seriously, since the direction of these factors have been arbitrarily set so that 'Aggressiveness' always loads negatively. Even ignoring signs, Table 3.6 demonstrates that the correlation between first factors is almost invariably the highest of the four. In the two classrooms where this is clearly not the case, both the between-factor correlations are higher than the within-factor correlations: there may well have been some cross-over effect of teachers' general valuation from first to second factor, or vice versa. But apart from these, the between-time factor correlations only seem to confirm the primacy of the first factor.

No attempt will be made here to provide a rigorous scheme for the

TABLE 3.6 *Correlations between first-year and second-year first and second principal components (subscripts refer to principal components, first year listed first)*

School(class)	r_{11}	r_{12}	r_{13}	r_{14}
Language programme				
11	0·742	0·046	−0·048	0·310
12	0·865	0·167	−0·041	−0·700
13	0·724	−0·300	0·323	0·713
Other working class				
22	0·756	−0·012	0·020	0·701
23	0·369	−0·182	−0·192	0·389
31	0·689	0·010	0·201	0·582
32	0·686	0·512	−0·453	0·620
33	0·492	0·609	−0·542	0·371
43	0·856	−0·021	0·089	−0·057
44	0·875	−0·284	0·187	0·775
Middle class				
51 (A)	0·818	0·286	0·042	0·151
51 (B)	0·655	−0·263	−0·362	−0·422
52 (A)	0·832	0·104	0·063	0·348
52 (B)	0·376	−0·615	0·687	0·053
53	0·702	−0·003	0·237	0·668
54	0·914	0·035	0·276	0·261
55	0·806	−0·166	−0·027	0·688

directional scoring of individual second rating-factors; as a result, correlations which involve second factors cannot be meaningfully pooled. However, while a full set of mean correlations from Table 3.6 is thus excluded, an analogous set obtained through an alternative measure of central tendency, the median, is not – as long as the signs are ignored. On this basis, the median first-factor stability is 0·74, the median second-factor stability is 0·42, and the two median between-factor correlations are 0·17 and 0·19 respectively. It is evident that a stable distinction between first and second factors is sustained by the different teachers over the two school years, and it is clear, too, that while the median first-factor stability is by far the highest of the four correlations, the median second-factor stability is sufficiently high for the second factor to merit some attention in this study. The directionality problem will prove to be a serious inhibitor in the proper examination of second factors, but a within-classrooms estimate from a matrix of pooled ratings will be briefly considered at a later stage.

Since the first factor is always assumed to be a general factor, the problem of direction does not arise, and first-factor stabilities may quite legitimately be treated to a conventional description of mean and variation. In the total sample, the stability of first rating-factors via pooled covariance matrices, i.e. taking factor variances into account, is 0·697; the stability via pooled *z*-values is 0·739. Of the individual ratings, only 'Brightness' can match these. The variation of covariance matrices is considerably larger than would be expected on a random sampling basis ($\chi^2_{48}=71{\cdot}25$, $p < 0{\cdot}01$), but the variation of *z*-values is not ($\chi^2_{16}=21{\cdot}13$), and there are no significant differences between groups of classrooms. Clearly the factor-variances, which are a direct function of factor loadings, provide all the significant variation. It is impressive that, despite great variability in the composition of first rating-factors, variation in the stability of those factors is sufficiently small to be entirely consistent with the null hypothesis of random sampling.

Estimates of a general factor covering both school years

Up to this point, the factor-rating relationships have been examined separately for the first and second school years. In keeping with factor analytic tradition, the formal comparison of repeated factors is shrouded in mystery. To avoid rushing in where wise men have so conspicuously failed to tread, the combination and comparison of repetitions will be characterised by simplicity, perhaps naivety. The first summarising tactic for all teachers, across times as well as across classrooms, is to use a simple repeated measures model, where y=rating and x=factor. Table 3.7 shows the correlation of each summed rating with the summed first factor and the proportion of summed rating-variance accounted for. Table 3.8 shows the variation between teachers of associated regression coefficients.

The statistics in these tables tell a now familiar tale. Just over half the pooled variance of summed ratings is explained by the pooled sum of first factors.[3] 'Aggressiveness' has become even less important, with only 10 per cent of its variance accounted for, while 'Brightness', 'Future school career' and 'Answering' have become still more dominant, with over 70 per cent of their variances accounted for. The variation between teachers of rating-on-factor regressions is what would be expected on a conventional random sampling basis for 'Brightness', 'Future school career' and 'Answering', but it differs significantly from the random sampling model for all other ratings. The consistent dominance of intellectual and academic elements in teachers' general valuation of children is dramatically emphasised.

The second summarising tactic is a rather unusual one. If the factor loadings in Tables 3.3 (i) and 3.3 (ii) are transformed into *z*-values, and the appropriate degrees of freedom (n-3) are taken into account,

TABLE 3.7 *Correlations, and correlations squared, between each rating summed over time and the first factors summed over time for the total sample (via pooled covariance matrices)*

	r	r^2
Explanation	0·627	0·393
Questioning	0·734	0·539
Answering	0·847	0·717
Aggressiveness	0·325	0·106
Independence	0·677	0·458
Attentiveness	0·714	0·510
Co-operativeness	0·662	0·438
Brightness	0·869	0·755
Future school career	0·868	*0·753*
Sum of r^2		*4·668*
Mean r^2		0·519

TABLE 3.8 *Variation (sums of squares=SS) between sample teachers in the regression of each rating summed over time on first factors summed over time, plus F-values and associated probability levels*

	Between classrooms		*Between teachers, within classrooms*		*Total Between teachers*	
	SS	$F_{16,249}$	SS	$F_{17,249}$	SS	$F_{33,498}$
Explanation	16·9	1·22	17·1	1·89*	34·0	1·48*
Questioning	12·2	1·27	20·7	1·89*	32·8	1·60*
Answering	6·7	<1·00	8·0	1·04	14·7	<1·00
Aggressiveness	54·7	2·87‡	20·9	2·59‡	75·6	2·75‡
Independence	46·4	4·42‡	18·1	2·10†	64·5	3·36‡
Attentiveness	27·8	2·50‡	10·8	1·42	38·6	2·05‡
Co-operativeness	29·5	2·38†	12·0	1·42	41·5	1·98‡
Brightness	8·2	1·24	3·7	<1·00	11·9	1·01
Future school career	8·6	1·36	3·9	<1·00	12·5	<1·00

* $= p<0·05$, † $= p<0·01$, ‡ $= p<0·001$

the result is a weighted items by times repeated measures set-up for group means. Altogether, there are $2 \times 9 \times 17 = 306$ z-values, which gives sufficient degrees of freedom to make analysis of variance a practical proposition. It should be added that no significance test on the variation of z-values between teachers is intended, since this variation is now the residual term. In fact, the between-teacher variation is very high, much higher than would be expected between z-values in a set of random samples. It is no surprise, then, that an analysis of variance on the total matrix of z-values reveals only one significant variation, namely that between the average z-values of individual ratings. Table 3.9 shows these average z-values transformed back into correlations, and Table 3.10 shows the between-teacher variation of z-values.

Except for some loss of sharpness, the results are extraordinarily similar to those in Tables 3.7 and 3.8, and so require no additional comment. Two quite different modes of summarising the rating-factor data across all teachers have produced virtually identical results, underlining both the value-orientation of the first factor and the dominance of intellect, academic future and speech quality in the composition of that value-laden factor.

It might be, however, that in the process of factoring every teacher, pooling all the first factors, and then summing these pooled factors across the two school years by whatever method, various relational distortions have crept into a final solution such as shown in Tables 3.7 and 3.9. For example, it has already been suggested that the first-factor loadings of most ratings vary considerably more than would be expected from a set of random samples, and it could well be that a

TABLE 3.9 *Correlations, and correlations squared, between each rating and first factors summed over time for the total sample (via pooled z-values)*

	r	r^2
Explanation	0·657	0·432
Questioning	0·724	0·524
Answering	0·828	0·686
Aggressiveness	0·367	0·135
Independence	0·698	0·487
Attentiveness	0·730	0·533
Co-operativeness	0·709	0·503
Brightness	0·863	0·745
Future school career	0·855	*0·731*
Sum of r^2		*4·776*
Mean r^2		0·531

TABLE 3.10 *Variation between sample teachers in the z-values derived from first-factor loadings*

	Between classrooms df = 16	*Between teachers, within classrooms df = 17*	*Total between teachers df = 33*
Explanation	63·0	44·6	107·6
Questioning	53·4	69·7	123·1
Answering	24·3	53·4	77·6
Aggressiveness	93·1	50·1	143·2
Independence	120·0	53·1	173·2
Attentiveness	68·6	48·2	116·8
Co-operativeness	92·1	39·3	131·4
Brightness	30·6	24·0	54·7
Future school career	28·0	23·9	51·9

number of relatively 'arbitrary' first factors, e.g. slightly larger clusters with relatively little value-content, have found their way into the overall characterisation of the first factor. Accordingly, there are good reasons for comparing the pooled first rating-factors summed over time with the first factor generated by a matrix of pooled correlations between ratings summed over time; the same matrix with which this examination of the rating-set was introduced in Table 3.1. The first principal component from that matrix is shown in Table 3.11, and because there are two latent roots greater than unity, the second principal component is also shown.

It is quite clear that, apart from accounting for slightly more set-variance, the first factor obtained from the correlations between pooled ratings summed over time is extraordinarily similar to the pooled first rating-factors summed over time. This is particularly so when the pooling and summation takes the route which produced Table 3.7. In fact, the correlation of the pooled first factor in Table 3.7 with the first factor in Table 3.11 is almost perfect ($r = 0{\cdot}974$), while that with the second factor in Table 3.11 is virtually zero ($r = 0{\cdot}030$). It need hardly be added that, once again, 'Brightness', 'Future school career' and 'Answering' dominate the first factor, and that 'Aggressiveness' is by far the weakest first factor correlate.

Besides providing some kind of check on the process by which a pooled first factor is obtained, a factor analysis of the matrix of pooled ratings presents the first real opportunity to examine an overall estimate of the second rating-factor. Again, the only rating

TABLE 3.11 *First and second principal components obtained from the pooled correlations between the sum of first- and second-year ratings for the total sample.*

	r		r^2	
	Factor 1	*Factor* 2	*Factor* 1	*Factor* 2
Explanation	0·658	−0·515	0·433	0·265
Questioning	0·757	−0·372	0·573	0·138
Answering	0·874	−0·136	0·764	0·018
Aggressiveness	0·371	−0·792	0·138	0·627
Independence	0·709	−0·179	0·503	0·032
Attentiveness	0·725	0·552	0·526	0·305
Co-operativeness	0·682	0·500	0·465	0·205
Brightness	0·878	0·209	0·771	0·044
Future school career	0·869	0·271	*0·755*	*0·073*
Sum of r^2			*4·926*	*1·754*
Mean r^2			0·547	0·195

which correlates more highly with the second than the first factor is 'Aggressiveness', and the difference is much sharper than that suggested by Table 3.4. 'Aggressiveness' is by far the strongest correlate of the second factor, but a few other ratings also figure prominently in its composition. These are 'Explanation' and, to a lesser extent, 'Questioning', which load in the same direction as 'Aggressiveness'; and 'Attentiveness' and 'Co-operativeness', which load in the opposite direction. Evidently the second factor describes active versus passive behaviour, and because the only categorial value-bias is located in the 'Attentiveness'/'Co-operativeness' end of the factor, there is a distinct implication that the passive behaviour, with its hint of submission to the teacher's authority, is more valued than the active. But while the second factor does imply a specific valuation, an underlying preference for one kind of behaviour over another, the first factor contains such an overwhelming mass of value-judgment that to interpret it as the factor incorporating the general valuation of teachers remains quite unchallengeable.

Differences between the LEAs

On a formal level, it has been justifiable to pool groups of teachers, for once the substantial between-teacher variations are taken into account, there are no significant differences between groups of teachers in terms of repeated factor patterns. However, a particular and rather powerful kind of significant difference between the working- and middle-class LEA teachers has arisen for two of the ratings. The relationship of 'Explanation' and 'Co-operativeness' with the summed factors declines significantly ($p < 0{\cdot}001$ and $p < 0{\cdot}01$ respectively) from first to second year in the middle-class LEA, and in both cases this change differs significantly from the working-class LEA (at the same probability levels).[4] It should be pointed out, though, that while the same trends are evident for *z*-values, they are very much weaker, never quite reaching the standard 0·05 significance level.

Nonetheless, it is illuminating to place these changes into some kind of general perspective by re-examining the factor-rating relationships, controlling for school year and for LEA. Table 3.12 shows the correlations between pooled within-time ratings and pooled first factors summed over time for the two LEAS; Table 3.13 shows the analogous factor loadings derived from pooled *z*-values.

TABLE 3.12 *Correlations between ratings within time and first factors summed over time for each* LEA *(via pooled covariance matrices)*

	Working-class LEA		*Middle-class LEA*	
	1st yr.	*2nd yr.*	*1st yr.*	*2nd yr.*
Explanation	0·472	0·574	0·752	0·347
Questioning	0·501	0·627	0·673	0·638
Answering	0·725	0·792	0·737	0·702
Aggressiveness	0·228	0·161	0·528	0·332
Independence	0·477	0·599	0·592	0·708
Attentiveness	0·605	0·627	0·717	0·578
Co-operativeness	0·532	0·636	0·690	0·409
Brightness	0·788	0·795	0·807	0·832
Future school career	0·778	0·797	0·745	0·816

The dominance of 'Brightness', 'Future school career' and 'Answering', and the comparative irrelevance of 'Aggressiveness' is a recurring feature in the working-class LEA. The middle-class LEA shows a similar pattern in the second year, though not quite so sharply, for 'Independence' loads as highly as 'Answering', and 'Explanation' and 'Co-operativeness' move closer to a less irrelevant 'Aggressiveness' at the bottom of the list.[5] But the first year in the middle-class LEA is quite different. For one thing, there is a remarkable uniformity of factor-rating correlations. For another, while 'Brightness' is still the highest factor-correlate, 'Explanation' has now moved up to the same level as 'Answering' and 'Future school career'. So the valuation of first-year teachers in the middle-class

TABLE 3.13 *First- and second-year factor loadings for the working- and middle-class* LEAs *(via pooled z-values)*

	Working-class LEA		*Middle-class* LEA	
	1st yr.	*2nd yr.*	*1st yr.*	*2nd yr.*
Explanation	0·622	0·664	0·796	0·526
Questioning	0·701	0·721	0·744	0·754
Answering	0·824	0·844	0·810	0·822
Aggressiveness	0·343	0·175	0·667	0·404
Independence	0·582	0·704	0·758	0·802
Attentiveness	0·701	0·766	0·737	0·698
Co-operativeness	0·647	0·772	0·770	0·601
Brightness	0·846	0·864	0·869	0·883
Future school career	0·839	0·869	0·831	0·878

LEA seems to be as powerfully oriented to quantity of teacher-directed speech as it is to the quality of that speech, or, for that matter, to the child's academic future.

If the correlation matrices from which the first rating-factors were derived are pooled for each LEA, the pattern of first-year teachers' ratings in the middle-class LEA sometimes diverges in a quite extraordinary fashion from that exhibited by the other three sets of teachers. Not surprisingly, the sharpest divergences are associated with 'Explanation' and 'Co-operativeness'. Two configurations in particular may be selected for presentation and comment. The first is the relational structure of 'Explanation', 'Questioning', 'Co-operativeness' and 'Attentiveness' as exhibited by each of the four sets of teachers, and this is shown in Table 3.14.

Three of the four matrices conform with the overall pattern already noted in Table 3.1, namely that there are two distinct, rather poorly correlated, clusters: 'Explanation' with 'Questioning' and 'Co-operativeness' with 'Attentiveness'. The first-year teachers in the middle-class LEA, however, appear to hold quite a different notion of what constitutes co-operative behaviour, for 'Explanation' and 'Questioning' correlate nearly as highly with 'Co-operativeness' as they do with each other, and 'Co-operativeness' actually correlates more highly with 'Explanation' and 'Questioning' than it does with 'Attentiveness'. In other words, 'Explanation'–'Questioning' has been joined by 'Co-operativeness' to become a clear three-variable cluster, with the consequence (i) that the usual 'Co-operativeness'–'Attentiveness' linkage is attenuated, and (ii) that, since 'Attentiveness' still has a large component in common with 'Co-operativeness', the correlation of 'Attentiveness' with 'Explanation' and 'Questioning' is somewhat higher than usual. So verbal approach to the teacher is clearly defined as co-operative behaviour by the first-year teacher in the middle-class LEA, but by no other group of teachers.

There are, then, powerful indications that the structure of teacher-pupil relationships is rather different for first-year infants in the middle-class LEA. It seems that children are encouraged to initiate interaction with the teacher, to be verbally active as well as fluent in their verbal reactions. The child has, on the face of it, much more control on the structure and content of classroom interactions, and, in that sense, the teacher culture may be seen as more child-oriented.

A further point should be made. Because the focus of teachers' valuation in the middle-class LEA has changed, at least to the point where hierarchies of importance are shifted and sharpened, an attenuation of first-factor stability might be expected. Not at all. The first-factor stability in the working-class LEA is 0·675, in the middle-class LEA it is actually higher at 0·749. The criteria may change, but the overall value-judgment, however arrived at, remains extraordinarily stable. It looks as though children who can gain a favourable definition from teachers by reference to a given set of criteria are also highly adaptable to changes in what constitutes a favoured disposition or behaviour.

Table 3.15 gives a remarkable demonstration of this apparent adaptability, and, in so doing, presents the second relational configuration which particularly distinguishes the two LEAS. It shows the pooled correlations between first-year 'Explanation' and all first- and second-year ratings in both the working- and middle-class LEAS.

TABLE 3.14 *Pooled correlations between 'Explanation', 'Questioning', 'Co-operation' and 'Attentiveness' in the working- and middle-class* LEAS *for the first and second school years*

		First school year					*Second school year*			
		Exp.	*Ques.*	*Co-op.*	*Att.*		*Exp.*	*Ques.*	*Co-op.*	*Att.*
Working-	Exp.	1·00				Exp.	1·00			
class	Ques.	0·71	1·00			Ques.	0·65	1·00		
LEA	Co-op.	0·12	0·19	1·00		Co-op.	0·37	0·39	1·00	
	Att.	0·09	0·15	0·77	1·00	Att.	0·26	0·32	0·74	1·00
		Exp.	*Ques.*	*Co-op.*	*Att.*		*Exp.*	*Ques.*	*Co-op.*	*Att.*
Middle-	Exp.	1·00				Exp.	1·00			
class	Ques.	0·76	1·00			Ques.	0·60	1·00		
LEA	Co-op.	0·66	0·70	1·00		Co-op.	0·08	0·33	1·00	
	Att.	0·46	0·45	0·59	1·00	Att.	0·09	0·37	0·69	1·00

TABLE 3.15 *Pooled correlations between first-year 'Explanation' and all first- and second-year ratings in the working- and middle-class* LEA*s*

	Working-class LEA		*Middle-class* LEA	
	1st yr. rating	*2nd yr. rating*	*1st yr. rating*	*2nd yr. rating*
Explanation	1·000	0·482	1·000	0·360
Questioning	0·712	0·320	0·762	0·482
Answering	0·524	0·380	0·552	0·504
Aggressiveness	0·392	0·328	0·529	0·400
Independence	0·179	0·275	0·332	0·479
Attentiveness	0·089	−0·006	0·464	0·364
Co-operativeness	0·120	0·024	0·658	0·257
Brightness	0·266	0·180	0·521	0·561
Future school career	0·248	0·172	0·422	0·549

The highest second-year correlate of first-year 'Explanation' in the middle-class LEA is not 'Explanation', as it most properly is in the working-class LEA, but 'Brightness' and then 'Future school career'. Incredibly enough, these correlations are actually higher than the correlations with first-year 'Brightness' and 'Future school career'. Children who, allegedly, talked a lot to teachers in the first year seem to have adapted to the change in second-year values by suddenly, mysteriously, becoming brighter, exhibiting a more rosy future school career and, relatively, inhibiting their propensity to talk to teachers, which is exactly what has not happened in the working-class LEA. Whether this apparent adaptability to changing teacher values is a special characteristic of classroom systems recruiting middle-class children obviously cannot be answered within the framework of this study, because the values of working-class LEA teachers seem to stay relatively constant. The point is that once a child is highly rated the child tends to stay highly rated, and among middle-class children at least, this is true irrespective of the changing relative importance of specific behaviours and dispositions.

Conclusion

The structure of the rating-set varies, in part, according to the where and when of the infant-school teacher's location. However, in terms of overall first-factor patterns, the variation between individual teachers is so great that the variation between groups of teachers is not, by conventional standards, inconsistent with the null hypothesis that they are a function of between-teacher variation. Despite this variability, 'Brightness', 'Future school career' and 'Answering' consistently dominate the first rating-factor, whereas the first-factor status of the one value-neutral rating, 'Aggressiveness', is uncertain and, on average, by far the lowest of all the ratings. It is true that first-year teachers in the middle-class LEA apparently differentiate much less clearly between individual rating-questions, but even here 'Brightness' has the strongest average relation to the first factor and 'Aggressiveness' has the weakest.

It seems, then, that when the infant-school teachers make generalised value-judgments about the children they teach, they are focusing primarily on the present intellectual and future academic capabilities of those children. In doing so, fluency of speech would be one important kind of evidence by which an infant's intelligence and academic potential is assessed. None of this would be very surprising in the middle or later stages of the educational process, but these children are only five and six years old. They have only just started at school. All the conventional wisdom about the liberal child-oriented structure of primary education may well seem adequate to the casual observer of classroom interactions, but when the crunch comes, even such a mild crunch as a researchers' questionnaire, the critical reference points in a teacher's valuation of infant-school children appear to be academic ones.

Notes

1 In each case, we used the Hendrikson-White program (FA5) on the IBM 7094 at Imperial College. All further calculations were done by hand.
2 This comment applies especially to both teachers in school 32, and to the first-year teacher in 52 (B). These are the only cases in which as many as four items load substantially higher on the second than the first principal component. Each rating-set falls into two distinct clusters, and, as a consequence, the centroid factor, which is a kind of average of the correlation matrix, looks quite different from the first principal component.
3 The extraordinary similarity between the summed rating-variance explained (Table 3.7), and the sums of explained rating-variance (Table 3.4), is actually a function of two equally powerful opposing tendencies. On the one hand, the variance explained by a pooled regression coefficient is always less than the sum of variances explained by individual regression coefficients; on the other hand, the explained variance of a

summed score is always greater in proportional terms than the sum of explained variances, unless there are negative correlations in the system.

4 The significant time–LEA interactions should be excluded from the total between-teacher variation of 'Explanation' and 'Co-operativeness' shown in Table 3.8. If this is done, the variation between teachers of the 'Explanation' regression on the first factor is no longer significant, though the F-ratio at 1·18 is still larger than that of 'Answering', 'Brightness', or 'Future school career'.

5 The relationship between 'Aggressiveness' and the first factor as shown in both Tables 3.11 and 3.12 has two notable characteristics: (i) It is considerably higher in the middle-class than the working-class LEA. (ii) It declines fairly sharply in both LEAS. However, the variation between individual teachers in their rating of 'Aggressiveness' is so large that neither of these visibly strong trends gets near conventional significance levels.

Chapter 4 Prediction of teachers' ratings

The first factor in the rating-set has been used to indicate what it is about children that the teacher considers valuable. It has been used to make inferences about teachers' primary reference points in their general valuation of children, but not how teachers arrived at those reference points, nor what kind of children benefit from the consequent valuation. The notion that a child brings typical behaviour displays to the classroom which the teacher measures through a rating-score is rejected as theoretically naive and politically subservient, for it tacitly assumes that teachers have an observational function which is detached, objective and free of individual or collective bias. A teacher's ratings do not indicate whether children have the alleged characteristics, only whether the teacher thinks they have. In order to assess what it is about children that influences a teacher's valuation, independent measures of children are necessary.

It would have been nice to use direct measures of child behaviour either in or out of the classroom, but it seems that the most 'scientific' method of obtaining such measures is through an observer with a check-list of behavioural categories. In principle, this has all the disadvantages of ratings made by teachers, and a study comparing teachers' ratings with researchers' ratings, however 'standardised' the researchers' observation and scoring procedures, reduces ultimately to a study in comparative biases. The child behaviours collected by the SRU sample are those which have been exhibited in various test situations, but they have been obtained mostly for smaller sub-samples of children. In fact, the only child-measures available over the total sample are the fairly standard ones relating to the child's intelligence and home background. In order to keep the projected analysis as simple as possible, a few of the more critical child-variables have been chosen for detailed consideration: sex, IQ, social class and the mother's communication and control pattern.[1]

Independent and dependent variables

The indices of parental social class and of mothers' orientation to communication and control are extensively described and analysed in Brandis and Henderson (1970). Both were constructed on the basis of information collected from the mother at the beginning of the child's school career. The Social Class Index is the sum of father's occupational status at the time of interview, the mother's occupational status before marriage, and the educational level of both father and mother. The Index of Communication and Control (ICC) is actually a composite of five separate indices, indicating the propensity of the mother (i) to continue a verbal interaction initiated by the child, (ii) to answer difficult questions from the child, (iii) to encourage exploratory behaviour in the child's relationship with toys, (iv) to adopt a reasoning strategy when the child transgresses, and (v) to avoid punishing the child in the same transgression situations. The characteristics of ICC depend a great deal on where it is applied. In the working-class LEA it is better predicted by social class and it is a better predictor of verbal IQ, particularly when controlling for social class. Its variance, as well as its power to discriminate, is noticeably reduced in the middle-class LEA. It should be added that the questionnaire from which the ICC was constructed was not given to mothers of children in the three working-class LEA control schools, and scores are not available for a few of the other mothers, so the ICC sample is considerably reduced.

The IQ data collected is set out in the introduction to this book. These data raise a problem. It could be that IQ scores are in some sense affected by teachers' definition of the child, more particularly since infant-school teachers appear to assign a particularly high value to children's intelligence. In order to keep the analysis as uncomplicated as possible, only the three IQ scores obtained at the beginning of the child's school life – Matrices, Crichton, and EPVT – will be used at this stage. All the variables to be used are therefore indirect measures of what the child has brought to school with him, and may in every sense be considered independent of teachers' ratings.

These measures will be treated as the independent variables in an analysis of covariance set-up, so interval scaling is assumed in each case.[2] In the text that follows, the first factor in each teacher's rating-set will be the dependent variable, and in the appendix to Chapter 4, the analysis is extended to the set of individual ratings after each teacher's first factor has been partialled out. Once again, the analyses are concerned not with differences between (adjusted) means, but with differences between relationships, in this case regression coefficients of ratings on child attributes. Residual variances will be used as error terms to assess how far between-teacher variation exceeds that expected on the basis of conventional random sampling. If the between-teacher variation may 'reasonably' be attributed to random sampling, it will be combined with the residual variance to become a pooled error term for tests of significance on the variations between groups of teachers, and/or a test of significance on the overall regression. If the attribution of between-teacher variation to the random sampling process is suspect, then it will become the new error term for these tests. The level of significance considered critical for the decision whether to pool or to substitute will be 0·10, since there need merely be doubt about the status of between-teacher variation, not the 'certainty' associated with the conventional 0·05 level.

The first principal component

Table 4.1 shows that analysis of covariance for each independent variable, with the first principal component from each first- and second-year teacher's rating-set treated as a repeated measures criterion. There are no significant differences between the pooled regressions of language programme and the remaining working-class LEA schools, so for the sake of presentational economy these are not shown.

Each independent variable is significantly related ($p < 0{\cdot}05$ or better) with the sum of first factors in all or part of the sample. At the same time, there are no relational differences between first- and second-year factors in the total sample. No matter which year at infant school, the whole sample of teachers gives higher ratings to girls, to children of relatively higher social class and to children of high IQ, irrespective of the tests used to produce the IQ scores. 'Relatively' higher social class because the social-class variation within classrooms is extraordinarily low, and this reflects the considerable social homogeneity of infant-school catchment areas. Not surprisingly, then, although social class has a significant effect on ratings, it is nowhere near as powerful as IQ; nor, for that matter, is sex. Of the IQ scores, the most powerful relationship with teachers' ratings is produced by the test of active verbal IQ, namely Crichton.

There is one highly significant difference between the pooled LEA regressions of summed factors, and that is on the Index of Communication and Control. It turns out that while the ICC has a powerful relationship with teachers' ratings in the working-class LEA ($p < 0{\cdot}001$), it has no relationship whatever with teachers' ratings

TABLE 4.1 *Analyses of covariance, partitioning degrees of freedom (df), and sums of squares of the first factor in the rating-set, into components due to regression on each of six independent variables. The difference between first- and second-year first factors is also partitioned into the regression components due to the sum of those factors. (x = independent variable, a =* LEA, *k = classroom, i = child and t = school-year; symbols in parentheses indicate nesting)*

Total Sample (*n* = 283. The ICC sample is reduced by 3 classrooms, 72 children, and *df* should be adjusted accordingly.)

Component	*df*	*Sums of squares*						
		Summed factors	*Sex*	*Social class*	*Matrices*	*Crichton*	EPVT	ICC
(i) Between classrooms (sum of first- and second-year factors)								
x	1		437*	551§	1692§	2668§	1620§	626
xa	1		126	47	18	33	3	309‡
xk(a)	15		882†	615	300	382	776†	451
i(xk)	249		9229	9460	8663	7590	8274	6965
(ii) Between teachers within classrooms (difference between first- and second-year factors)								
tx	1	5	7	0	11	0	0	10
txa	1	59*	27†	9	14	31*	12	24
txk(a)	15	181*	119	74	106	142	164†	107
ti(xk)	249	1663	1756	1825	1777	1735	1733	1210

* = $p<0{\cdot}05$, † = $p<0{\cdot}1$, ‡ = $p<0{\cdot}01$, § = $p<0{\cdot}001$

in the middle-class LEA. This, in fact, could be interpreted as a description more of the ICC than the ratings, for it merely emphasises the lack of ICC's power to discriminate between socially hierarchical attributes in the middle-class LEA. Not surprisingly, the highly-rated child in the working-class LEA is the one whose mother's overall communication and control score most resembles that of mothers in the middle-class LEA (see also p.122).

Other significant differences between pooled LEA regressions do appear, but they are all differences in the difference between the first-year and second-year factors. Differential change from first to second school years is associated with the sum of first factors, with Crichton, and with sex, in that order. In each case, the association becomes stronger in the working-class LEA and weaker in the middle-class LEA, though neither change manages to reach the 0·05 significance level in its own right for any of the three variables. Now the correlation between a sum of two scores and their difference is a simple function of the difference in their variances. In other words, the size of the first factor increases in the working-class LEA and decreases in the middle-class LEA, a differential change which is significant despite a significant departure from the random sampling model in between-teacher within-LEA variation. It could well be, then, that the differential change noted in the regressions on other independent variables are a function of changing criterion variances. Accordingly, Table 4.2 shows the difference between factors controlling for the sum of factors, i.e. the 'controlled' change, explained by the six independent variables.

TABLE 4.2 *Analyses of covariance. partitioning degrees of freedom, and sums of squares of the difference between first- and second-year first rating-factors, with the sum of those factors partialled out in each classroom, into components due to regression on each of six independent variables (component symbols as in Table 4.1)*

Components	*df*	*Sums of squares, controlling for summed first factors*					
		Sex	*Social class*	*Matrices*	*Crichton*	EPVT	ICC
tx	1	1	4	8	1	2	0
txa	1	8	6	9	4	2	7
txk(a)	15	62	107	60	106	142	94
ti(xk)	232	1592	1547	1586	1552	1518	1095

NOTE The probability of any term in the first three rows appearing by chance is always greater than 0·10.

As a result of this control, every significance has vanished. Once the summed factors are partialled out of the difference between the factors, all observed changes from first to second year may be attributed to the sampling process. It should be added, however, that this does not necessarily constitute an adequate explanatory system. What ultimately requires explanation is the differentially changing factor-variances to which the differentially changing relationships between independent variables and factors have been imputed. It could well be argued that the different cohesions between ratings which ultimately produce the different factor-variances are themselves a consequence, either wholly or partly, of different strengths of reference to particular sets of child characteristics, such as those represented by the child-measures used in this study. In other words, it is quite possible, on a substantive level, to reverse the explanatory order implied by the exercise which produced Table 4.2 (this line of argument is explored in some depth by Bernstein in Part II of this book).

Finally, the variation between classroom regressions of summed factors may be examined. It is surprising, considering the heterogeneity of factor-rating correlations, that the effects of only two independent variables show any noticeable departures from the random sampling model. These are sex and EPVT, and the variation of between-classroom within-LEA regressions for each only manages to reach the 0·10 significance level. If the resulting non-significant variation between pooled LEA regressions is added in, the between-teacher variation for EPVT no longer even reaches 0·10, but that for sex is now clearly significant at 0·05. While girls, on average, obtain a significantly higher rating than boys in the infant school, there is some quite pronounced variation between classrooms in the rating-status occupied by girls.

However, sex is a bit of a problem. There is evidently rather more variation between pooled LEA regressions than would conventionally be expected, but the substitution of a marginally significant between-teacher within-LEA variation for the usual residual term renders it completely non-significant. The trouble is that everything is borderline. In order to strive for a clearer solution, the regression of summed ratings on sex may be controlled by partialling out the best predictor of summed ratings, which is Crichton.

TABLE 4.3 *Analysis of covariance, partitioning degrees of freedom, and sums of squares of first factors summed over time, into components due to regression on sex, plus the same analysis after Crichton is partialled out in each classroom (component symbols as in Table 4.1)*

	Uncontrolled		*Controlling for Crichton*	
Components	*df*	*Sums of squares*	*df*	*Sums of squares*
x	1	437*	1	331
xa	1	126	1	159*
xk(a)	15	882†	15	603
i(xk)	249	9229	232	6497

* $= p < 0{\cdot}05$, † $= p < 0{\cdot}10$

Table 4.3 shows that this simple control completely reverses the configuration of significance. The between-teacher within-LEA variation of regressions due to sex does not even reach the 0·10 significance level, whereas the variation between pooled LEA regressions has actually increased. Accordingly, the decision to substitute is superseded by a decision to pool, and as a result the relationship between sex and summed first rating-factors is now clearly significant at the 0·05 level. Girls are rated significantly more highly than boys in the middle-class LEA ($p < 0{\cdot}001$), but in the working-class LEA the slightly higher rating of girls falls well within the limits of conventional sampling error.

In summary, teachers are remarkably consistent in their general rating-policies when it comes to picking up social and intellectual cues from the children, and this is particularly apparent if a few simple statistical controls are exercised. No matter how much the first rating-factors may vary in composition, it is the same kind of children who consistently obtain high first-factor scores from teachers. High IQ children are given consistently high ratings in both LEAS, and, less emphatically, so are children from relatively higher social backgrounds. This consistency is maintained within LEA even when there is a clear difference between LEAS in the rating-practice of teachers, as in response to the child's sex and the mother's communication and control pattern, where there is no sex discrimination in the working-class LEA but girls are highly rated in the middle-class LEA, and the converse holds for children with high ICC mothers.

By examining the relationship between child-attributes and teachers' ratings within an analysis of covariance framework, the discussion so far has necessarily emphasised statistical significance rather than relational magnitude. This may be corrected by pooling the correlations associated with the analyses of covariance. In deference to the LEA–ICC and (controlled) LEA–sex interactions, the pooled correlations shown in Table 4.4 are kept separate for the two LEAS.

Two general comments may be made. First, while there is little difference between the regressions of first rating-factor on IQ, the associated correlations are distinctly lower in the middle-class than the working-class LEA. One reason is that IQ variances are reduced in the middle-class LEA: in the case of EPVT, which is the only standardised IQ score, the difference in variances is significant at the 0·02 level. The second point concerns the LEA-specific predictors of teachers' ratings. ICC correlates highly with the first rating-factors in the working-class LEA, but not as highly as the three IQ tests (at least not in the reduced ICC sample). Moreover, the moderately high relationship between ICC and verbal IQ does suggest that a component shared by both measures is in part responsible for the size of the relationship between ICC and teachers' ratings. Sex, on the other hand, is completely independent of IQ, and only one IQ test, Crichton, manages to obtain a higher relationship with the first rating-factor

TABLE 4.4 *Pooled correlations between six independent variables and first- and second-year first rating-factors*

	Sex	*Home background*		*IQ test scores*			*First rating-factor*	
		Soc. class	ICC	*Matrices*	EPVT	*Crichton*	*1st year*	*2nd year*
(i) Working-class LEA *(10 classrooms, 184 children)*								
Sex	1·000							
Social class	−0·090	1·000						
ICC	−0·016	0·400	1·000					
Matrices	−0·084	0·189	0·150	1·000				
EPVT	−0·079	0·229	0·250	0·383	1·000			
Crichton	0·056	0·213	0·271	0·351	0·558	1·000		
1st year rating	0·066	0·261	0·351	0·381	0·407	0·517	1·000	
2nd year rating	0·166	0·255	0·426	0·436	0·396	0·527	0·675	1·000
(ii) Middle-class LEA *(7 classrooms, 99 children)*								
Sex	1·000							
Social class	−0·027	1·000						
ICC	−0·236	0·229	1·000					
Matrices	−0·023	0·133	0·126	1·000				
EPVT	0·005	0·345	0·285	0·180	1·000			
Crichton	−0·017	0·225	0·100	0·121	0·640	1·000		
1st year rating	0·331	0·181	0·028	0·285	0·297	0·380	1·000	
2nd year rating	0·293	0·089	−0·042	0·283	0·249	0·296	0·749	1·000

NOTE (*a*) ICC sample is reduced by 3 schools, 69 children in the working-class LEA, and by 3 children in the middle-class LEA. If the ICC sample is taken in the working-class LEA, all correlations between independent variables and ratings go up. (*b*) Sex is scored so that female is equivalent to a 'high' score.

than sex in the middle-class LEA. This is the only instance in which a variable genuinely independent of IQ has been found to relate just as powerfully to teachers' ratings as IQ does.

Apart from the influence of sex in the middle-class LEA, it is evident that IQ is by far the most powerful general predictor of teachers' ratings in the infant school. Indeed, the correlations between IQ and first rating-factors are very high by any standards. When correlations of this order appear between two measurement procedures which have so little in common, and when they refer to children sufficiently young to ensure that the upper limits of measurement consistency are bound to be depressed, the researcher may be excused for wondering if the discourse of validity is more appropriate than that of causality. The IQ scores in this study had no effect on teachers' ratings, for the teachers did not know them. Any inference has to go back to what an IQ test is supposed to be measuring. A teacher's rating-score, whose primary reference points are intellectual and academic, has an unusually powerful relationship with tests that their producers and, indeed, whole social systems, think are measures of intelligence. Neither score could have influenced the other, so inferences have to be made from the measures to what it is that is being measured. The point at which the interpretation of a relationship must graduate from conventional prediction, with its implied causality, to validity is where the inferred variables cannot be distinguished from each other. So if substantially the same dimension is being measured by IQ tests and by the first factor of teachers' ratings, a causal inference would simply reduce to the utterly meaningless statement that intelligence (or whatever it is) produces intelligence. These speculations, and what they imply, will be considered more systematically in Chapter 5.

Factors in the pooled ratings

When the composition of the first rating-factor was being examined, it was suggested that some distortion might arise from factoring each teachers' rating-set and pooling the results. This was checked in a very general way by factoring the pooled ratings summed over time, which had the additional advantage of allowing a second factor to be explored, though with the proviso that no account was, by definition, being taken of between-teacher variation. For much the same reasons, and with the same reservations, the relationship between independent variables and factors derived from the pooled ratings summed over time may be considered. Table 4.5 shows how the independent variables correlate with the first and second principal components derived from the pooled ratings summed over time (see Table 3.11) and, for comparison, how they correlate with the pooled first rating-factors summed over time (see Table 3.7).

TABLE 4.5 *Total sample correlations of independent variables with pooled first rating-factors summed over time (pooled factors), and with the first and second principal components obtained from the pooled ratings summed over time (within-classroom factors)*

	Sex	*Social class*	*Matrices*	*Crichton*	EPVT	ICC
Pooled first factors	0·202	0·227	0·398	0·500	0·390	0·242
Within-classroom first factor	0·185	0·232	0·401	0·505	0·400	0·257
Within-classroom second factor	0·103	0·169	0·156	0·063	0·145	0·042

A number of points may be noted. First, the correlation of any independent variable with the first factor derived from pooled ratings is very much the same as that with the pooled first rating-factors, though all variables except sex correlate a little more strongly with the former. Second, the second rating-factor correlates positively with all the independent variables, but in every case, this correlation is weaker than with the first rating-factor. Third, IQ is by far the most powerful determinant of the first rating-factor, no matter which IQ test or which total sample estimate of a first factor is used, but IQ has no special role in the determination of the second rating-factor, and is indeed slightly superseded by social class.

It is evident that the first factor dominates the rating-set, not only in terms of the proportion of variance accounted for, but in terms of its simple predictability by IQ, social background and sex. It is also clear that while the second factor is very much a subsidiary dimension in the rating-set, the direction in which it correlates with every single independent variable confirms the valuation inferred from the distribution of value-biased rating-categories. Children who come from a relatively higher social background, children with a generally higher IQ, and girls are all rated as more deferential to the classroom order which centres on the teacher. These are precisely the children who obtain high scores on the first rating-factor. The distribution of self-evidently value-biased rating-categories in both factors fits exactly with the social value-judgments carried by the independent variables.

There is a strong case, then, for arguing that the first principal component in this particular rating-questionnaire is not entirely efficient in picking up the full force of teachers' valuation. Had the analysis omitted 'Aggressiveness', 'Explanation' and 'Questioning', i.e. each of the ratings in which the net effect of the rating-categories is value-neutral, the result would have been to rotate the first factor towards 'Attentiveness'/'Co-operativeness', probably transforming the 'Brightness' and 'Future school career' loadings on the second factor to zero. As a consequence, relationships of independent variables to second factor would fall, some perhaps becoming negative, and relationships to first factor would generally tend to rise. However, the practical effect on first-factor relationships would be so small that the naked eye would have great difficulty in detecting any change at all. In short, even if the first factor were rotated to correct the bias which may be inferred as arising from the inclusion of rating-questions without value-biased categories, it would still remain primarily an IQ-determined factor.

Parenthetically, it may be noted that the two variables whose correlations with the second rating-factor are closest to zero, Crichton and ICC, are also the two variables with a strong verbal activity component in them. The reason for this seems to be that, apart from its promotional function in the generation of academic success, there is an underlying disapproval of verbal activity in the infant classroom on strictly behavioural grounds. Verbal activity does not receive a blanket approval in the way that being attentive or co-operative does. It is approved behaviour only in so far as it is perceived to have intellectual/academic implications, and when these implications are absent it is disapproved of, almost certainly on the grounds that, like being aggressive, it is disruptive of the classroom order. In that sense, 'Aggressiveness', 'Explanation' and 'Questioning' all appear to be double-valued, with the positive valuation entirely contingent on the teacher's perception of their intellectual/academic content.

In general, there are good reasons why the second rating-factor ought not to be ignored. It has a median classroom stability of 0·42, it has the only other within-classroom latent root greater than one, and it has moderately high correlations with some of the independent variables; but on all counts it is a much less important factor than the first. Moreover, the manner in which the second factor was obtained has allowed no estimate of between-teacher variations, and so it has not been possible to test whether the relationships examined apply throughout the whole sample or whether they are specific to particular groups of teachers.[3] This exploration of the second factor has been useful, for it has indicated that there is another, though very subsidiary, value-system in the rating-set, and at the same time it has highlighted the intellectual/academic orientation of the first factor. But apart from this, comments on the structure and determinants of the second rating-factor should, at least in terms of their generalisability, be treated as strictly tentative.[4]

The full ratings

In mapping the relationship between independent variables and rating-set, each rating has been partitioned into common and unique components; the contributions made to first (and second) principal components, and the residuals which remain after the principal components have been partialled out (see appendix to Chapter 4). It remains only to add them together and observe the relationships between uncontrolled ratings and independent variables. These are shown in Table 4.6.

TABLE 4.6 *Pooled correlations for the total sample between each teacher's rating summed over time and six independent variables, plus the correlation of every item with pooled first factors summed over time*

	Sex	*Social class*	*Matrices*	*Crichton*	EPVT	ICC	*First factors*
Explanation	0·173	0·079	0·138	0·329	0·186	0·114	0·627
Questioning	0·148	0·086	0·240	0·427	0·299	0·153	0·734
Answering	0·126	0·211	0·367	0·442	0·364	0·235	0·847
Aggressiveness	−0·058	−0·091	0·023	0·110	0·012	0·054	0·325
Independence	0·042	0·138	0·262	0·239	0·139	0·181	0·677
Attentiveness	0·214	0·238	0·373	0·419	0·373	0·164	0·714
Co-operativeness	0·234	0·168	0·285	0·349	0·268	0·126	0·662
Brightness	0·172	0·268	0·392	0·461	0·411	0·274	0·869
Future school career	*0·117*	*0·294*	*0·436*	*0·468*	*0·443*	*0·315*	*0·868*
First factors	0·202	0·227	0·398	0·500	0·390	0·242	1·000

All the correlations are positive, except for 'Aggressiveness' with sex and social class. Indeed, 'Aggressiveness' is always the lowest correlate, while at the other end, 'Future school career' and 'Brightness' have the highest correlations with all independent variables except sex, where 'Co-operativeness' and 'Attentiveness' are the highest correlates. In general, the correlations between teachers' ratings and independent variables reflect the factor-rating correlations with some accuracy, and it is clear that the listing of correlations with successive ratings does, in large part, involve a persistent repetition of correlations with the first principal component.

Above all, Table 4.6 emphasizes once again the powerful overall relationship in the total sample between teachers' ratings and IQ, particularly Crichton. This test is the best predictor of every single rating except 'Independence', where it is superseded by Matrices. Even the second-best predictor is almost invariably one of the three IQ tests, and so, usually, is the third-best predictor. It is evident that teachers' ratings, whether taken singly or soaked up in a first factor, are closely moulded to the intelligence measured by conventional IQ tests.

Notes

1 In fact, other background variables such as family size, ordinal position and overcrowding have actually been used in the analysis, but they add little or nothing to what is explained by the variables selected. In order to keep explanations as simple as possible, no further reference will be made to them.

2 A scale called sex might horrify some practitioners. One of the rules of thumb which abound in applied statistics is that a correlational scale should have something like ten points in it at least. However, those who would religiously avoid putting sex into a correlation will happily divide a sample into male and female for analysis of variance. As it happens, the two techniques produce exactly the same results.

3 It has already been shown, for example, that the rating policy of first-year teachers in the middle-class LEA differs considerably from that of other teachers in the sample, particularly when it comes to differentiating between 'Co-operativeness' and 'Explanation'/ 'Questioning' (see Table 3.14). Predictably, the second factor for this set of teachers looks quite different from that which has been obtained for the total sample of classrooms.

4 The common component with which this study is concerned has been a source of some uneasiness. By definition, the halo effect is something that is common to two or more ratings. The analysis here has tended to proceed on the basis that the first principal component in the total rating-set constitutes a fair representation of the halo effect. Since halo effect, however, is essentially valuational in character, it could justifiably be argued that the common component which best represents the halo effect should not have been identified by reference to the full rating-set, but by reference to the subset which consists of ratings exhibiting a clear categorial value-bias. In short, 'Aggressiveness', 'Explanation' and 'Questioning' might be related to the halo effect, but should not have been directly used in the identification of that halo effect. One practical

way of dealing with this difficulty might be to rotate the first and second principal components extracted from the full rating-set such that the resulting first principal component accounts for the maximum variance only in the subset of the six value-biased ratings. This would have several interesting consequences. It would tend to reduce the variation between the first rating-factors of different teachers, and it would also produce a second factor which could be pooled by reference to the common directionality of the three ratings that are categorially value-neutral. The overall importance (=factor loading) of 'Co-operativeness', 'Attentiveness', 'Future school career' and 'Brightness' would increase; that of 'Answering' and 'Independence', as well as of the three value-neutral ratings, would decrease. The correlations between first-factor and background variables would tend to rise only marginally, but a somewhat different pattern of significant relationships between rating-residuals and background variables would emerge. In general, the net effect of taking the first principal component in the full rating-set as the halo-induced component has almost certainly been to introduce a variable and thoroughly unhelpful bias, and thus to make the analysis less elegant and its interpretation more complicated than might have been.

Chapter 5 Teachers' ratings and intelligence

This study has been economical in its selection of variables. When ratings, or, indeed, any other item-sets, are factored by computer, as they now invariably are, it is customary for factors to proliferate, perhaps as an insurance against allowing minor quirks in the correlation matrix to slip away. Yet the whole point of factoring is to economise in the description of the item-set. Again, the ready availability of multiple regression programmes with huge capacities has resulted in massive prediction studies with every kind of independent variable thrown in, just in case. The student may have noticed how an expansion in the number of variables studied generally results in rapidly diminishing marginal returns of increasingly dubious inferences. What, perhaps, is not so clear is how a proliferation of variables can easily obscure a central relationship which is critical to some of the phenomena being studied. No apologies are made here for expending so many resources on disentangling the relationships between so few variables.

The rating-set in this study has been looked at in three ways: the consistency of single ratings, the structure of the first rating-factor, and the prediction of ratings from a few selected child-attributes. The superior consistency exhibited by infant-school teachers in their ratings of 'Brightness' and 'Future school career' has introduced, and serves to emphasise, the inference from first factors that teachers value intellectual and academic qualities above all others. To drive the point home, the most powerful external correlate of this inferred valuation is the child's IQ. Because everything seems to revolve around intelligence, the IQ-rating relationship may be subjected to a more thorough examination.

Verbal IQ, non-verbal IQ and teachers' ratings

So far, relationships have been traced between three sets of IQ scores, obtained during the first few weeks at infant school, and the first rating-factors of two different teachers, one at the end of the first year and the other at the end of the second. These particular IQ scores were used in order to pre-empt the possibility that ratings may have affected IQ. However, the relationship between initial IQ and subsequent ratings is so high that the prediction orientation, with its implied causality, which guided the selection of those tests, may well be less than adequate in capturing the full flavour of the IQ-rating relationship. At the beginning of the second school year, the WISC was administered to all children in the working-class LEA, and a shortened form consisting of four sub-tests was administered to all children in the middle-class LEA. If the same four sub-tests are selected from the working-class LEA, a fairly standard set of IQ scores at the beginning of the second school year is available for the total sample.

The total short-form WISC consists of two verbal sub-tests, 'Similarities' and 'Vocabulary', and two clearly non-verbal (performance) sub-tests, 'Block design' and 'Object assembly', so the short-form total may be split into a verbal and a non-verbal IQ score. Of the initial IQ tests, two are verbal and one is non-verbal, but the verbal EPVT correlates more highly with Matrices and WISC performance, and less highly with WISC verbal, than Crichton does. So Crichton appears to be the 'purer' verbal IQ. If EPVT is omitted on the grounds of its slightly less certain verbal status, two verbal and two non-verbal tests remain. Each set of scores within either test category has been obtained from a different IQ test, and there is a year's interval between them. This matches nicely with the teachers' ratings situation, since each rating-set has been obtained from a different teacher and there is a year's interval between them. The only disjunction is one of times-measures, for both kinds of IQ scores were obtained at the beginning of the school year, whereas ratings were obtained at the end. As a consequence, the relationship between verbal and non-verbal IQ should be increased in relation to that between both kinds of IQ and teachers' ratings, and the fact that the verbal-non-verbal split of the second-wave IQ is derived from the same test should serve to accentuate this disparity.

It has been established that there is no difference between classrooms in the regression of first rating-factors on any of the initial IQs. Nor is there any difference between LEAs in these regressions, but a reduction of IQ variances in the middle-class LEA does help to produce a substantial drop in the associated IQ-rating correlations. Table 5.1 shows the pooled within-classroom variances of the three initial IQs and the WISC verbal and non-verbal IQs in each LEA.

Every IQ variance is lower in the middle-class than the working-class LEA, a difference which is significant for EPVT ($p < 0{\cdot}02$) and marginally so for WISC verbal ($p < 0{\cdot}10$). Now Crichton and Matrices

TABLE 5.1 *Pooled within-classroom variances of five* IQ *tests in the middle-class and working-class* LEAs, *and the* χ^2*-value (df = 1) derived from Bartlett's test for the significance of the variance differences between* LEAs.

	Initial IQ tests			Short-form WISC	
	Matrices	*Crichton*	EPVT	*Verbal*	*Non-verbal*
Working-class LEA	11·994	40·592	209·077	32·045	28·759
Middle-class LEA	10·033	31·920	130·871	22·627	22·446
χ_1	0·93	1·61	6·16*	3·45†	1·78

* = $p < 0{\cdot}02$, † = $p < 0{\cdot}10$

are non-standardised raw scores, WISC verbal and non-verbal are both non-standardised sums of two standardised sub-tests ($\mu = 10$, $\sigma = 3$), and EPVT is a fully standardised test ($\mu = 100$, $\sigma = 15$). The degree of standardisation in verbal and non-verbal tests is schematically shown in Table 5.2, together with the χ^2-value which indicates the difference between the two LEA variances.

TABLE 5.2 *Verbal and non-verbal* IQ *tests by degree of standardisation, plus the* χ^2*-value indicating the reduction of observed within-classroom variance in the middle-class* LEA *compared with that in the working-class* LEA

Standardisation	*Non-verbal tests*	*Verbal tests*
None	*Matrices* $\chi^2 = 0{\cdot}93$	*Crichton* $\chi^2 = 1{\cdot}61$
$\mu = 10$, $\sigma = 3$ (component sub-tests)	WISC *short form* $\chi^2 = 1{\cdot}78$	WISC *short form* $\chi^2 = 3{\cdot}45$
$\mu = 100$, $\sigma = 15$		EPVT $\chi^2 = 6{\cdot}16$

It is clear that verbal tests always exhibit more between-LEA differences in variances than non-verbal tests do, and that this difference increases in both verbal and non-verbal tests as the degree of standardisation (and, for that matter, the variance itself) becomes greater. The closer a test approximates to the theoretical norms which are thought appropriate for IQ tests, the greater the comparative reduction of within-classroom variance in the middle-class LEA.

EPVT has already been excluded from the selected IQ tests on the grounds that it is not as verbal a test as Crichton, but the implication is that all IQ tests, and verbal tests in particular, will exhibit attenuated relationships in the middle-class LEA. Accordingly, the scheme of two verbal IQ tests, two non-verbal IQ tests, and two first rating-factors should be looked at separately for the two LEAS. Table 5.3 shows the pooled within-classroom correlations between the six variables for each LEA.

TABLE 5.3 *Pooled correlations between two verbal* IQ *tests, two non-verbal* IQ *tests, and two teachers' ratings (first factors) for each* LEA

Working-class LEA ($n = 182$)

	Non-verbal IQ		*Verbal* IQ		*First rating-factor*	
	Matrices	WISC	*Crichton*	WISC	*1st yr.*	*2nd yr.*
Matrices	1·000					
WISC non-verbal	0·560	1·000				
Crichton	0·342	0·368	1·000			
WISC verbal	0·324	0·397	0·627	1·000		
1st yr. rating	0·384	0·440	0·522	0·483	1·000	
2nd yr. rating	0·438	0·438	0·532	0·476	0·674	1·000

Middle-class LEA ($n = 99$)

	Non-verbal IQ		*Verbal* IQ		*First rating-factor*	
	Matrices	WISC	*Crichton*	WISC	*1st yr.*	*2nd yr.*
Matrices	1·000					
WISC non-verbal	0·351	1·000				
Crichton	0·121	0·164	1·000			
WISC verbal	0·127	0·150	0·483	1·000		
1st yr. rating	0·285	0·151	0·380	0·350	1·000	
2nd yr. rating	0·283	0·129	0·296	0·431	0·749	1·000

As expected, all correlations involving IQ tests are lower in the middle-class than the working-class LEA, though it should be added that they are not especially lower for verbal tests. This is, however, the only real difference between the two LEAS, and there are some surprisingly consistent patterns across the two correlation matrices.

In all, four major points may be noted. First, the highest correlation for any variable in either LEA is always with its one-year match, as indeed it is supposed to be. Second, the highest correlation in each matrix is always between the two first rating-factors, so the one-year stability between teachers is always higher than the one-year stability between any IQ tests.[1] Third, verbal IQ tests always have a higher consistency than non-verbal tests, and verbal tests always correlate more highly than non-verbal tests with the first rating-factors. Finally, any IQ score always correlates more highly with the first rating-factors than with scores from the other IQ group; the only exception is the non-verbal WISC in the middle-class LEA, which clearly has difficulty in correlating with anything at all. So verbal and non-verbal IQ actually correlate more highly with the teachers' ratings than they do with each other.

This is a quite extraordinary configuration of relationships. If the last two variables in the matrix had not been labelled 'teachers' ratings', but another set of IQ scores incorporating both verbal and non-verbal elements, then, given the relational structure of the first four variables, the correlation matrices would have been shrugged off as unexceptional. If, alternatively, the last two variables had been a third kind of IQ score, with the same formal status *vis-à-vis* general intelligence as verbal and non-verbal IQ, then they would have been regarded as the most powerful measures of general intelligence in the set. In short, the first factors of the teachers' ratings are behaving not merely as if they were IQ tests, but as if they were the most powerful IQ tests in the set.

An application of the bi-factor method

These comments may be given a more formal character by applying a factor analytic technique, the bi-factor method,[2] which is intended for precisely the kind of relational patterns shown in Table 5.3. It is designed to account for an observed correlation matrix by reference to a general factor plus a series of non-overlapping group factors. Given a generally positive correlation matrix which divides into three or more fairly neat clusters, the correlations between the clusters can be interpreted as a direct function of a general factor, and the residual correlations within the clusters a direct function of various orthogonal group factors, one for each cluster. After the general factor has been partialled out, the between-cluster residuals should be approximately zero, whereas the within-cluster residuals should still be fairly large. If there is overlap between the two sets of residuals, and particularly if any between-cluster residuals are statistically significant, or any within-cluster residuals are virtually zero, the factor plan should be adjusted so that the offending elements are properly allocated. When, after suitable adjustments, the group-factors are partialled out of the residual matrix, the final residual matrix may be tested for the factor-plan's goodness of fit. Harman (1967) suggests that the standard deviation of the residual correlations should be somewhat less than the standard error of a zero correlation for that sample size.

Cluster analyses of the two matrices in Table 5.3 indicate what is already obvious to the naked eye – that there are three two-variable clusters in each matrix. The correlations between, but not within, verbal IQ, non-verbal IQ and first rating-factors, may then be attributed to a general factor defined by all the six variables. As the clusters are all doublets, unique group-factor coefficients cannot be determined from the general factor residuals, but in this instance the determination of group factor coefficients is a fairly marginal issue. Table 5.4 shows the general factor derived from each matrix, and the residual matrices are shown in Table 5.5.

TABLE 5.4 *General factor coefficients from the three-cluster bi-factor plan for each* LEA

	Working-class LEA		*Middle-class* LEA	
	r	r^2	r	r^2
Matrices	0·522	0·272	0·311	0·097
WISC non-verbal	0·578	0·334	0·246	0·060
Crichton	0·663	0·440	0·477	0·227
WISC verbal	0·638	0·407	0·505	0·255
1st yr. rating	0·761	0·579	0·753	0·566
2nd yr. rating	0·786	0·617	0·730	0·533
Sum of r^2		*2·649*		*1·738*

Before the substance of the general factors is examined, a glance at the residual matrices shows that they account extraordinarily well for the between-cluster relationships. All within-cluster residuals are higher than between-cluster residuals, and each one of the latter is well below the standard error of a residual correlation with one factor removed. Five of the six within-cluster residuals are well above the same standard errors; the exception is first rating-factors in the working-class LEA, where the residual falls just below the standard error. The status of this particular clustering is therefore a little uncertain, so the factor-plan could be adjusted by designating the two first rating-factors as separate, one-variable, clusters. However, re-calculating the general factor on this basis results in only very marginal changes: the explained IQ variance falls by about 1 per cent and the explained first rating-factor variance rises by about 4 per cent.

The differences between initial and adjusted solutions in the

TABLE 5.5 *Residual matrices after partialling out the general factor in the bi-factor plan for each* LEA

Working-class LEA *(standard error of residual r = 0·087)*

	Non-verbal IQ		*Verbal* IQ		*First rating-factor*	
	Matrices	WISC	*Crichton*	WISC	*1st yr.*	*2nd yr.*
Matrices	—					
WISC non-verbal	0·258	—				
Crichton	−0·004	−0·015	—			
WISC verbal	−0·009	0·028	0·204	—		
1st yr. rating	−0·013	0·000	0·017	−0·003	—	
2nd yr. rating	0·028	−0·016	0·011	−0·025	0·076	—

Middle-class LEA *(standard error of residual r = 0·142)*

	Non-verbal IQ		*Verbal* IQ		*First rating-factor*	
	Matrices	WISC	*Crichton*	WISC	*1st yr.*	*2nd yr.*
Matrices	—					
WISC non-verbal	0·274	—				
Crichton	−0·027	0·047	—			
WISC verbal	−0·030	0·026	0·242	—		
1st yr. rating	0·051	−0·034	0·021	−0·030	—	
2nd yr. rating	0·056	−0·051	−0·052	0·062	0·199	—

working-class LEA are not very large, and, no matter which is used, the general factor in the working-class LEA accounts for considerably more variance than that in the middle-class LEA.[3] This is particularly so for the IQ scores, though it should be added that there is less IQ variance to be accounted for in the middle-class LEA. There are, however, no other major differences between the two LEAS. In each case, the first rating-factors are by far the highest correlates of the general factor, followed by the verbal IQs, and last the non-verbal IQs. If all or part of the component common to verbal and non-verbal IQs is construed as general IQ, then any factor which accounts for the linkage between those two kinds of IQ must be taken to account for general IQ. A self-evident rule in the identification of factors is that the highest empirical contributors receive the greatest weight, so the general factor which describes the links between verbal IQ, non-verbal IQ and teachers' ratings is primarily a teachers' ratings factor. In short, a general factor identified principally by reference to teachers' ratings accounts entirely for general IQ.[4]

Taken at face value, this stands the classic prediction model on its head. How can teachers' ratings account for general IQ? Teachers cannot rate children until the children come to school, yet pre-school children can be meaningfully differentiated in terms of IQ scores. Obviously, teachers' ratings cannot possibly have any part in the determination of pre-school IQ. And if, as current established belief would have it, IQ is largely a fixed genetic quantity, then teachers' ratings can have very little effect on IQ at any time. Proponents of the classic model are in the dilemma that what is measured by IQ tests must not merely have determined teachers' ratings, but over-determined them to the point where IQ appears to be a function of teachers' ratings. In order to side-step such an awkward position, it might be useful to explore a wider explanatory perspective.

The social link between IQ tests and teachers' ratings

The measurement of human behaviour, or of human dispositions to behave, is an academic exercise carried out under the umbrella of the human sciences, but it is also a persistent feature of the social systems which those sciences purport to study. It is not surprising that the distinction between the two is often slight, that social scientists in general, and test constructors in particular, take socially defined behavioural categories as part of their starting-point, and feed more or less revised behavioural categories, plus devices with which to measure them, back into the social system. Looked at in this way, a social system's psychology-culture, or, for that matter, its sociology-culture, is quite as legitimate an object of academic enquiry as its teacher-culture. The part of psychology-culture which is concerned with the measurement of intelligence is socially defined as 'scientifically' superior to a teacher-culture which might pretend to do the same, but this is precisely a social valuation, and in that sense the products of psychology-culture cannot be given more *a priori* credence than the products of any other culture. Certainly, by supplying social systems with more and more selection mechanisms, the academic psychology-culture is at many points so closely interwoven with the wider social structure that the sociologist cannot afford to ignore its status as a vital part of social systems.

It would not be so surprising, then, if the inventors, administrators, analysts and interpreters of IQ tests place a similar construction on the notion of intelligence as that exhibited by teachers, such that teachers are merely one of many social groups who are integrated in a general, IQ-focused, culture. But even if the teachers' and psychologists' notions of what constitutes intelligence are virtually identical, it would not explain how teachers' ratings come to be dominant in accounting for general intelligence. The shape of the general factor suggests almost that a series of different IQ scores, with varying reliabilities and slightly more bias to the verbal than the non-verbal, have been absorbed by the teachers and averaged out in the first principal component of the teachers' ratings. This would make sense if the classroom situation were visualised as a constant process of implicit testing, with fragmentary test-situations widely and persistently sampled from a general intellectual domain (however defined), and their results coagulating into an increasingly more confident and stable definition of the child. In short, the teachers would be able to produce a more general and consistent measure of intelligence because they can average out, as it were, more test results, even though formal IQ tests might never have been administered. On this argument, the classroom situation is the direct social extension of the IQ test. By the same token, the IQ test is a sampling and formalisation of the processes which characterise the classroom situation.[5]

This clears up an important unresolved issue. Up to now, the first factor in the rating-set has been used to indicate the value-system of infant-school teachers, and the consistency across behavioural and dispositional rating-dimensions which might have been present irrespective of measurement procedure has largely been ignored. By interpreting the first rating-factor as another IQ test, the rating is not just a valuation in which conventional intelligence is a critically important referent, but a direct measure of that intelligence in its own right. It seems hardly necessary to add that the intelligence of the teachers' ratings, like the intelligence of the psychologists' IQ tests, functions both as a description and as a value judgment.

If teachers' ratings are, in effect, the most powerful IQ tests in the set, then IQ-correlates external to the set should correlate even more highly with teachers' ratings. This is precisely what happens in the working-class LEA, for sex, social class and ICC each correlate more highly with the first rating-factors than with the IQ scores. But it does not happen in the middle-class LEA. The home background variables, social class and ICC, both tend to correlate less highly with the first rating-factors than with the IQs, whereas sex, which has no relationship whatever with IQ, has by far the most powerful relationship with first rating-factors. In the middle-class LEA, then, teachers' ratings are relatively background-independent, but highly biased towards girls. Clearly, the middle-class first rating-factors have something more in them than IQ, especially when the fairly substantial consistency-residual is considered. Since the discriminatory power of IQ tests, purely in terms of variance, is visibly reduced in the middle-class LEA, it is conceptually somewhat problematical whether teachers' ratings have gained something extra or IQ tests have lost something. If anything, the IQ tests' loss of power in accounting for general IQ suggests that the latter is more likely, that the IQ of the psychologists is a more potent discriminator between working-class than middle-class children, whereas teachers retain their power to discriminate across the whole social spectrum. At all events, the general argument should perhaps be applied a little less wholeheartedly to the middle-class than the working-class LEA.

Apart from this qualification, it is important to disentangle what the line of reasoning adopted here does and does not imply. In the first place, it does not necessarily indicate which of the two groups, teachers or psychologists, is independent and which is dependent, or whether and to what degree they co-exist in a long-term interdependence wherein each group is constantly influencing the other's notion of what intelligence is and what its behavioural indicators are. It could even be that teachers' notions of what constitutes intelligence faithfully mirrors, with due cultural lag, the psychologists' ever-expanding theoretical advances in definition and measurement. Maybe if psychologists had rated the children under the same conditions as the teachers, the relationship between an intelligence rating-factor and various IQ tests would have been even higher. If that were to happen, it would be particularly interesting to see whether the intelligence factor derived from psychologists' ratings had the same generality over the rating-set as that obtained from the teachers' ratings. Second, while the non-academic social connections of IQ have been emphasised, the results in themselves generate no firm inference about the relative weights of genetic and environmental components in IQ. After all, infant-school teachers may be wonderfully skilled at extracting the genetic component from their perception of children's classroom behaviour, and making it the general anchor for their ratings of 'Brightness', 'Future school career', 'Answering', 'Questioning', 'Attentiveness', 'Independence', 'Co-operativeness', etc, etc.

However, what the results do emphasise is that teachers' ratings and IQ tests are substitutable, not just as measures of whatever it is they are measuring, but as potential selective devices in the educational system. If there were a political controversy about modes of selection at infant-school level, then the classic 'tests versus teachers' arguments would appear. The findings in this paper suggest that the winner of the great debate would have little or no substantive effect on the selection of children, since both 'alternatives' are overwhelmingly oriented to the same dimension, a widespread and consistent notion of intelligence which is inextricably part of the educational system at its earliest stages.

Notes

1 It could be argued that the comparison is unfair, since the short form of the WISC is bound to be less reliable than the complete test. Full WISC scores are available only in the working-class LEA, and if these are substituted for the short form, the consistency of verbal scores does increase to 0·676, which is almost exactly equal to the consistency of teachers' ratings, but that of non-verbal scores actually reduces to 0·553. On the other hand, there is a large increase in the relationship between WISC performance and the verbal tests, which suggests that the full-form WISC performance has a considerable verbal component. By way of confirmation, the WISC manual shows the correlations between the ten WISC sub-tests administered to 200 children aged 7½, and if the first two principal components in this matrix are rotated to a varimax (orthogonal) and then to a promax (oblique) solution, it becomes evident that while the verbal subtests have little non-verbal contamination, the reverse most certainly does not hold. Although the published correlation between the WISC verbal and performance IQs is 0·60, the correlation between the two promax factors is only 0·52. Two of the five performance subtests, 'Picture completion' and 'Picture arrangement', appear to suffer from substantial verbal contamination, and a third, 'Coding', is handicapped by a small communality. 'Block design' and 'Object assembly' are the only two Performance subtests which have an exclusive relationship with (inferred) performance IQ analogous to that between the five verbal subtests and (inferred) verbal IQ. There is overwhelming evidence, then, that the short-form WISC performance IQ is a much 'purer' test of non-verbal IQ than its fully expanded form.

2 The bi-factor method is described in Harman (1967), Chapter 7.

3 Though the two LEAs have been kept separate, this analysis has got itself into precisely the situation castigated earlier; there are no estimates of between-classroom variations, so there are no proper criteria by which formal comparisons can be made between LEAs. The major reason for this is a combination of factoring method and sample size, for samples of fifteen and twenty exhibit relational distortions which, though attributable to sampling fluctuations, are sometimes too large to be accommodated by the pre-set factor plan or an acceptable adjustment of it. It is, nonetheless, interesting to note that the general factor accounts almost completely for the consistency between teachers' ratings in the working-class LEA, but there is a respectably-sized residual of teachers' ratings consistency in the middle-class LEA. There is, then, plenty of room in the middle-class LEA for the special and persistent relationship between an IQ-independent sex and teachers' ratings.

4 Even if the criteria governing the choice of IQ tests are relaxed, and EPVT is included as an extra verbal test, there is only a slight narrowing of the differential general factor-loadings. The same is true if, in addition, the WISC short-form scores are split into their constituent sub-tests. In each case, the first rating-factors are still the principal identifiers of the general factor which accounts for the link between the three clusters.

The only other way to tinker with the basic design is in the working-class LEA, where the full WISC IQs may be substituted for their present short-form representatives. Note 1 indicates that the full WISC performance IQ contains a powerful verbal component, but the full WISC verbal IQ does not seem to have a corresponding non-verbal component. Accordingly, the latter may be substituted for its short-form equivalent without seriously affecting the appropriateness of the factor-plan. The general factor that results from this new matrix shows, once again, a marginal narrowing of differential factor loadings, with, predictably, the full WISC verbal IQ accounting for considerably more variance (about 12 per cent more) than its short-form equivalent. But even so, it does not correlate as highly with the general factor as either of the first rating-factors do. There is only one way in which any IQ tests can be made to supersede the first rating-factors, and that is by substituting the full WISC performance IQ on the pretence that it is a pure non-verbal test (which it certainly is not), and inserting the EPVT, on the pretence that it is a pure verbal test (which again it is not). If that is done, the consequent general factor accounts for about 5 per cent more of WISC IQ variances than of first rating-factor variances, though the three original IQs still remain considerably less important. In summary, no matter how much the criteria governing the choice of IQ tests are relaxed, the general factor in either LEA always correlates more highly with the first rating-factors than with matrices, Crichton, EPVT or either of the WISC short forms. Only the substitution of an absurdly contaminated full WISC performance IQ and the inclusion of EPVT in the working-class LEA is capable of raising any IQ tests above the level of the first rating-factors, and one of the two tests so raised is precisely the contaminated WISC performance. It is illuminating that under properly controlled conditions, the other of these two tests, namely the full WISC verbal IQ, cannot account for the link between verbal and non-verbal IQ as well as either of the first rating-factors can. This implies very strongly that had the full WISC performance been a purer non-verbal test composed, say, of five sub-tests such as 'Block design' and 'Object assembly', its contribution to the general factor would have been less than that of either first rating-factor.

5 For the benefit of those convinced that they are being subjected to a gigantic statistical and interpretive sleight of hand, a conventional description might at least serve to emphasise the remarkable power of the relationship between IQ and first rating-factor. It has already been noted that the full WISC, which was administered only in the working-class LEA, is the most extensive and powerful IQ test in the SRU repertoire. Despite considerable variability in the composition of first rating-factors, the correlation between full WISC total IQ and first rating-factor in the *average* working-class LEA infant classroom is 0·59 for first-year teachers and 0·61 for second-year teachers. An average correlation of 0·60 between two variables which are logically so unconnected should persuade even the most sceptical that a relationship of extraordinary importance is being discussed.

Appendix to Chapter 4
The residual ratings

In Chapter 4 a number of attributes which the children had brought to school with them were used to predict the first principal component in each first- and second-year teacher's ratings. These principal components may be partialled out from their respective rating-sets to leave a set of rating-residuals for each teacher, and the rating-residuals may in turn be subjected to the same kind of analysis as that performed on the first factors. In consequence, a second repeated measures component is introduced to the criterion in the covariance model, namely a repeated ratings term to cover the nine residuals where previously there had been only one factor. Unfortunately, a problem which has already been encountered in the examination of repeated scores does arise here in particularly acute form. As a direct consequence of differential factor-rating relationships, the residual variances differ considerably in size, so whether any differential relationship of independent variable with residuals achieves statistical significance rather depends on how far the larger residuals are involved. Significance tests associated with differential relationships should therefore be treated with some caution.

Independent variables and the rating residuals

None of the six independent variables relate significantly to the criterion, summed both over residuals and over times in all or part of the sample. Nor do five of them relate to the between-time difference of summed residuals. The one exception is sex. There is a significant difference ($p < 0{\cdot}05$) between the pooled LEA regressions of the change over time of summed residuals on sex, the change itself being significant in the working-class LEA ($p < 0{\cdot}05$). What happens is that girls in the working-class LEA tend to get generally 'higher' ratings, controlling for first factor, in the second year than in the first year.

Interestingly enough, the pattern for regressions of first-factor differences on sex is very much the same, but the difference between pooled LEA regressions, and the change regression in the working-class LEA, only manage to reach the 0·10 significance level, both vanishing completely when the summed factors are partialled out. On the other hand, if a straight sum of uncontrolled ratings is taken for each school year, exactly the same pattern of significance occurs, but this time all at the 0·01 level, and there are no significant differences between the individual ratings in the relationship of their change to sex. Table A1.1 shows how the correlations between sex and full ratings change over the two school years within each LEA.

TABLE A1.1 *Pooled correlations between sex and (uncontrolled) teachers' ratings for each* LEA */school year*

	Working-class LEA		*Middle-class* LEA	
	1st yr.	*2nd yr.*	*1st yr.*	*2nd yr.*
Explanation	0·082	0·156	0·365	0·034
Questioning	0·004	0·164	0·237	0·146
Answering	0·085	0·059	0·232	0·144
Aggressiveness	−0·160	−0·045	0·156	−0·051
Independence	−0·123	0·032	0·113	0·277
Attentiveness	0·093	0·203	0·266	0·267
Co-operativeness	0·072	0·241	0·326	0·257
Brightness	0·050	0·130	0·327	0·258
Future school career	−0·019	0·102	0·240	0·221

The increase in the rating-status of girls in the working-class LEA is, within the conventional limits of sampling fluctuation, uniform across all ratings. Girls start off receiving an average rating no higher than boys, but their relative position improves on virtually every rating by the end of the second year at school. Clearly the first principal component does not pick up the nuances of changing sex-rating relationships in the working-class LEA very efficiently. Girls are generally more highly rated in the middle-class LEA, but it is evident that girls in the working-class LEA are also moving in a blanket way towards the same superior status.

Apart from this local disturbance of principal component efficiency, there is one significance that occurs with no less than four of the six independent variables, and that is in the differential relationship with the nine residuals. There are no classroom interactions, no pooled LEA interactions, no time interactions, and no important combinations of these:[1] the differential relationships are significant over the total sample of classrooms and times. Significance is produced by sex ($p < 0{\cdot}05$), social class ($p < 0{\cdot}001$), Matrices ($p < 0{\cdot}01$) and EPVT ($p < 0{\cdot}01$). Only ICC and Crichton produce a spread of relationships with the residuals which may be attributed to random sampling – on what is, admittedly, a far from perfect test for this kind of data. The correlations associated with the residual variations due to regression on each independent variable are shown in Table A1.2.

'Aggressiveness' has by far the largest residual variation of the ratings, so any departures from non-significance in that particular residual tend to contribute disproportionately to an overall variation between the residuals. Thus, the 0·001 significance achieved by social class in its differential relationship to the residuals may in part be attributed to the outsize contribution of 'Aggressiveness', in terms not so much of its statistical significance, but of its sheer absolute size. It should be added that whenever 'Aggressiveness' contributes to a significant differential relationship of residuals with an independent variable, there are always other fairly powerful contributors. For instance, 'Future school career' makes some moderately large contributions in absolute terms despite the fact that it has the smallest variance to be accounted for.

This way of looking at Table A1.2 raises an interesting point. Certain residuals collect persistently significant correlations, and the directions of these are almost invariably the same. The most striking example is 'Future school career', with three correlations significant at the 0·01 level and one at the 0·05 level. Other prominent residuals operating this way are 'Aggressiveness', 'Independence' and 'Brightness'. The significant relationships with 'Future school career' and 'Brightness' are all positive, those with 'Aggressiveness' and 'Independence' are all negative. Yet 'Future school career' and 'Brightness' already have the highest relationship with the first factor, which in turn correlates positively with all the independent variables, and 'Aggressiveness' has the lowest. If the first factor's relationship with 'Future school career' and 'Brightness' had been even higher, and its relationship with 'Aggressiveness' and 'Independence' even lower, then these persistent unidirectional significances would not have occurred. The implication is that the differentials between factor-rating relationships have been flattened over the total sample, either because the principal component is not completely efficient in picking up a socially-determined teachers' valuation, or because the structure and composition of this particular rating-questionnaire would impair the efficiency of any summarising technique.

For one of the ratings, however, there is a different and entirely plausible inference. 'Future school career' is the outstanding collector

TABLE A1.2 *Pooled sums of squares (SS) of each rating-residual summed over time, plus the pooled correlations between six independent variables and each summed rating-residual, for the total sample*

		Correlations with independent variables					
	SS	*Sex*	*Social class*	*Matrices*	*Crichton*	EPVT	ICC
Explanation	208·1	0·036	−0·068	−0·136*	0·026	−0·048	−0·063
Questioning	133·8	−0·014	−0·105	−0·060	0·109	0·037	−0·081
Answering	111·1	−0·037	0·047	0·066	0·062	0·085	0·016
Aggressiveness	283·6	−0·127*	−0·176†	−0·122	−0·033	−0·095	0·022
Independence	156·0	−0·106	0·010	−0·030	−0·135*	−0·192†	0·059
Attentiveness	160·8	0·098	0·110	0·118	0·066	0·060	−0·092
Co-operativeness	179·0	0·124*	0·020	0·020	−0·005	−0·051	−0·082
Brightness	100·4	0·032	0·141*	0·106	0·085	0·148*	0·085
Future school career	97·7	−0·090	0·189†	0·188†	0·088	0·195†	0·161*

* = $p < 0·05$, † = $p < 0·01$

of significances, and it is also the only rating which makes a prediction. Teachers could well be predicting that in the later stages of the educational process, IQ and social origin biases will become even greater than those which the infant-school teachers have themselves demonstrated in their ratings. It can be argued that 'Future school career' contains a prediction, in part, of future teachers' ratings, and that these future ratings are seen as merging still more closely with the IQ and social background of the child. By this argument, the occasional significance of the 'Brightness' residual may be viewed as a function of its very close relationship with 'Future school career'.

But such an interpretation does nothing to account for the other significant relationships in Table A1.2, and these may now be listed in more detail. The relationship between independent variables and the 'Aggressiveness' residual is generally negative, and it achieves conventional significance with sex and social class. Just as boys are judged especially aggressive, so girls are judged especially co-operative. These special ascriptions are not particularly startling, for they do conform to readily available social stereotypes about boys, girls and 'lower-class' children. The remaining significant relationships are rather more enigmatic: children with low verbal IQ (EPVT, Crichton) are judged especially independent, and children with low non-verbal IQ (matrices) are described as explaining things to teacher with special frequency. Whether all or some of these should be considered as separate specific relationships to be accounted for in face-value terms, or as a set consequent on a slightly adrift factorial solution, remains problematical.

Residuals in the pooled ratings

Just as the correlations of independent variables with pooled first factors have been checked against those with the within-classroom first factor, so the correlations of independent variables with the pooled residuals may be checked against those with the within-classroom residuals. Furthermore, it is possible that a number of significant relationships shown in Table A1.2 would vanish if a second factor were controlled for; and without a rigorous scheme for matching second factors across samples, the only way to explore this possibility is to control for the principal components derived from a pooled correlation matrix, with the important proviso that no estimate of between-teacher variation is then possible. Table A1.3 shows the correlations between independent variables and teachers' ratings controlling for (i) the first within-classroom principal component and (ii) both the within-classroom principal components.

TABLE A1.3 *Correlations between independent variables and the rating-residuals left after the removal of within-classroom principal components*

(i) Controlling for first principal component

	Sex	*Social class*	*Matrices*	*Crichton*	EPVT	ICC
Explanation	0·068	−0·098	−0·167†	−0·004	−0·102	−0·073
Questioning	0·012	−0·138*	−0·098	0·069	−0·006	−0·064
Answering	−0·074	0·016	0·035	0·002	0·029	0·021
Aggressiveness	−0·137*	−0·191†	−0·136*	−0·083	−0·146*	−0·044
Independence	−0·126*	−0·037	−0·031	−0·169†	−0·206‡	−0·001
Attentiveness	0·116	0·102	0·119	0·077	0·121*	−0·032
Co-operativeness	0·148*	0·014	0·016	0·007	−0·007	−0·067
Brightness	0·021	0·134*	0·083	0·038	0·125*	0·100
Future school career	−0·089	0·186†	0·178†	0·059	0·192†	0·186†

(ii) Controlling for first and second principal components

	Sex	*Social class*	*Matrices*	*Crichton*	EPVT	ICC
Explanation	0·189†	0·024	−0·084	0·053	−0·004	−0·060
Questioning	0·086	−0·050	−0·011	0·127*	0·093	−0·048
Answering	−0·047	0·066	0·081	0·021	0·073	0·034
Aggressiveness	−0·093	−0·089	−0·004	−0·056	−0·043	−0·016
Independence	−0·104	0·006	0·009	−0·158†	−0·174†	0·010
Attentiveness	0·056	−0·056	−0·010	0·044	0·007	−0·109
Co-operativeness	0·105	−0·140*	−0·124*	−0·051	−0·146*	−0·131
Brightness	−0·028	0·067	0·016	0·012	0·070	0·096
Future school career	−0·174†	0·111	0·111	0·029	0·135*	0·196†

* = $p<0·05$, † = $p<0·01$, ‡ = $p<0·001$

The relational network between independent variables and the residual pooled ratings shown in Table A1.3 (i) is very similar to that between independent variables and the pooled residual ratings shown in Table A1.2. Once again, significant relational spreads are produced by EPVT ($p<0·001$), Social class ($p<0·001$), Matrices ($p<0·001$) and Sex ($p<0·01$), while the patterns associated with ICC and Crichton may be attributed to chance. Without itemising every single significant relationship, it may be noted that, as before, the 'Aggressiveness' and 'Independence' residuals collect persistently negative correlations, while the 'Future school career' and 'Brightness' residuals collect persistently positive ones. Apart from a slight reshuffling across the lines of statistical significance, the overall relationships between independent variables and ratings controlling for the first principal component are remarkably steady, no matter how that principal component is estimated for the total sample.

When the second principal component is also partialled out of the pooled ratings, however, there are substantial changes in the patterns of significance. Significant relational spreads are now achieved by sex ($p<0{\cdot}01$), EPVT ($p<0{\cdot}01$), and Crichton ($p<0{\cdot}05$), but not by social class, ICC or Matrices. The mass of significant relationships associated with the 'Aggressiveness' residual has disappeared, as have those associated with 'Brightness'. On the other hand, a number of significant relationships do remain, and some new ones emerge.

Perhaps the most striking configuration of significance that remains is between the 'Independence' residual and verbal IQ. EPVT and Crichton both achieve significant relational spreads, and, in both cases, the strongest correlation is a negative one with the 'Independence' residual, which clearly plays a critical part in the generation of that significance. The difficulty with interpreting this relationship is in knowing what the independence is from in the teacher's head. Maybe the independence that teachers see is a propensity towards self-generated rather than other-generated behaviour, implying some measure of autonomy from the conventional process of verbal instruction and reasoning. But whether this imputed independence inhibits the acquisition of a high verbal IQ, or whether a low verbal IQ facilitates the development of such independence, must remain completely problematical.

A second residual that still correlates significantly with some independent variables is 'Future school career'. Children whose mothers have a high ICC score, or who themselves obtain a high EPVT score, are given a specially favourable academic prognosis, and so (non-significantly) are those with high Matrices scores or from a relatively higher social class. This may be explained in the same terms as before, that the social and intellectual bias already exhibited by teachers is thought likely to become even more pronounced as the child grows older. Of special note is the high correlation with ICC: it seems that, in the teachers' opinion, a characteristically middle-class, person-oriented, communication and control style on the part of the mother is likely to pay particularly high academic dividends in the child's later school life. Apart from these now familiar positive correlations, the 'Future school career' residual has also picked up one powerful and important negative correlation. Boys are rated as likely to do especially well in their school career compared with girls. This relationship is important because it exhibits the infant teachers' awareness of the sex bias which is built into the later stages of the formal educational system. It thus demonstrates that the 'Future school career' rating cannot simply be classified as a super-charged measure of the valuation contained in the first rating-factor. 'Future school career' clearly has a descriptive component all its very own, and this lends credence to the argument that the infant teachers are describing what they think is likely to happen to the child by virtue of his IQ and home background.

One other residual has emerged with persistently significant correlations, and that is 'Co-operativeness'. Oddly enough, all the significant correlations are negative. Children from a relatively higher social class, and children with a high Matrices or EPVT score, are all judged as being especially unco-operative. This is exactly the opposite to what is implied by the relational complex centring on the second factor. Possibly what has happened is that the value-component of the 'Co-operativeness' rating has been absorbed into the second factor, whereas its descriptive component has not. If that is the case, then high social class and high IQ children are considered 'better behaved', but not, in a purely descriptive sense, particularly co-operative.

Apart from the persistent significances associated with the 'Independence', 'Future school career', and 'Co-operativeness' residuals, there are two other significant correlations in Table A1.3 (ii): sex with 'Explanation', and Crichton with 'Questioning'. Girls are described as explaining things to teacher with special frequency, and this suggests two different though not incompatible inferences, which, in turn, may each be offered either as the teacher's definition of the social situation in the classroom or as the observed behavioural consequences of a social structure that the children bring with them to the classroom. It may be that the teachers, all female, are, or define themselves as, especially accessible to little girls by virtue of their shared sex, and/or it may be that boys are, or are defined as, inhibited from chattering to any adult figures because such 'indulgence' is not compatible with the little male role. The other significant relationship is much more straightforward. Children with a high score on the Crichton are described as asking teacher questions with special frequency. This relationship barely requires any comment, for it is only to be expected that a high active verbal IQ is associated with a generally questioning style, even if that association exists merely in the teacher's head.[2]

An attempt has been made to provide some sort of explanation for every correlation with the final rating-residuals that achieve statistical significance, but the quality of these explanations is perhaps not always what it ought to be. In order to place Table A1.3 into contextual perspective, it might be added that although a fair number of the correlations are significantly different from zero, none are particularly large. It is evident that neither the second rating-factor nor the rating-residuals can be predicted by the independent variables with the kind of assurance that the first rating-factor can be. Every single correlation with the final rating-residuals, or, for that matter, with the second rating-factor, is less than 0·20, whereas all but one of the correlations with the first rating-factor is greater than 0·20. A few relationships shown in Table A1.3 are interesting and even suggestive; others continue to be puzzling, and, within the context of this study, they are simply not large enough to warrant the explanatory ingenuity which is sometimes demanded.

Notes

1 The only significant variation produced by independent variables is in the most basic interaction of all: the residual × time × classroom (within-LEA) interaction, which is significant for social class ($p<0{\cdot}05$) and marginally so for ICC ($p<0{\cdot}10$). A time × classroom interaction is simply the controlled variation between teachers, so different teachers appear to attach somewhat different consequences, in terms of different rating-residuals, to home background. This interaction does not affect the tests of significance used on the differential relationship with rating-residuals.

2 A much tidier solution is obtained by simply partialling out the first principal component after it has been rotated to the solution suggested in note 4 of Chapter 4. The resulting 'Future school career' residual correlates significantly with five of the six background variables, namely ICC, Social class, EPVT, matrices and (negatively) sex. Only four correlations out of the remaining forty-eight achieve conventional significance: 'Independence' with EPVT (the only correlation to surpass the 0·01 level of significance), 'Questioning' with Crichton, 'Aggressiveness' with social class, and 'Co-operativeness' with sex. This relational pattern supports the argument that the persistent significances associated with particular rating-residuals in Tables A1.2 and A1.3 (i) are for the most part a consequence of the non-halo bias in the first principal component, and it also supports the 'substantive' explanation given for the significances associated wiht the 'Future school career' residual.

Part II Social class and teachers' models of the infant-school child

Basil Bernstein

Chapter 6 Teachers' ratings and the model of the infant-school child

Introduction

As we outlined in the introduction, in this section of our report we shall examine differences between the teachers in the middle-class and working-class area in how they rate the children at the end of the first and second years of the infant-school stage. For the sake of convenience we shall designate these two years as time I and time II. This analysis will examine in some detail the relationships between the social-class position of the child's family, an index of maternal communication and control, the sex of the child and the child's measured ability to the teachers' ratings. We have tried to clear this text of technicalities and our analysis is based upon a comparison of the size of various correlations and upon the pattern which we consider they form. We shall not in every case indicate levels of statistical significance, but we shall give the various levels of significance required for the samples in the working-class and middle-class area. We shall, of course, indicate when the difference between the size of any pair of correlations is statistically significant.

We must first explain what we mean by the teachers' model of the successful infant-school child. In Part I we described how all the teachers' ratings were factor analysed and a general factor obtained. (This general factor, the first factor, accounts for over 50 per cent of the variance.) This general factor represents an underlying common dimension to the ratings. Now when we look at the correlation between any individual rating with this general factor, we can obtain an idea of the relative importance of each individual rating to the general factor. If, for example, 'Aggressiveness' is weakly related to the general factor, then we take this to mean that children who are judged highly aggressive by their teachers are *less* likely to be considered 'successful' infant-school pupils. On the other hand, if an individual rating, like 'Explanation', is very highly associated with the general factor, we take this to mean that a child who, the teacher judges, offers explanation spontaneously and frequently to the teacher, is very likely to be judged a 'successful' infant-school child. We shall derive the teachers' model from the relative size of the correlation between individual ratings and the general factor. Thus, if we find that a correlation changes markedly between the first year and second year, or that a different trend appears either between the two areas or between the first year and second year, then we shall argue that there has been a change in the relative importance of the components (the ratings) of the teachers' model. We shall leave until the final section of the discussion questions about the origin and stability of the teachers' model of the 'successful' infant-school child. In simple terms, we are saying that teachers value certain general activities, certain specific competencies, certain attitudes, certain styles of work in the children, and the model shows their relative significance, their relative importance to the concept of the successful pupil.

The structure of the teachers' ratings

We shall first examine the ratings to see the behaviour of the pupil the teacher was asked to judge. There are three linguistic measures. Two of these are concerned with the frequency of initiated communication to the teacher ('Explanation' and 'Questioning'), and one which is more subject to teacher control ('Answering'). In the latter case, the child is *replying* to the teacher, and the teacher is assessing the adequacy of the pupil's answer in terms of its fluency. It may be that in the teacher's mind fluency is confounded with accuracy.

There are a group of four ratings, 'Aggressiveness', 'Independence', 'Attentiveness', and 'Co-operation', which at a very general level are concerned with the adequacy of the pupil's social relationship. Within this group we can distinguish at a general level 'Aggressiveness' and 'Independence' from 'Co-operation' and 'Attentiveness'. The first pair refers more to child-initiated behaviour, whereas the second pair refers to more teacher-controlled or focused behaviour.

There are two ratings which differ from the preceding seven: the ratings of 'Brightness' and the child's 'Future school career'. These ratings are different from the preceding seven for they are global estimates rather than estimates of specific competencies or specific behaviours. We also know that 'Brightness' and 'Future school career' are very highly correlated (see later section) in both areas and at both times, so that 'Brightness' is a major factor in the teacher's judgment of a future favourable school career. As we shall see later, the children's measured ability is very highly correlated with the teachers' judgments of the degree of 'Brightness' of the child.

We can group these ratings as follows:

1 Linguistic cognitive measures — child-initiated: 'Explanation', 'Questioning'; teacher-controlled: 'Answering'

2 Measures of the adequacy of the child's social relationship — child-initiated: 'Aggressiveness', 'Independence'; teacher-controlled: 'Co-operativeness', 'Attentiveness'

3 Cognitive measures: 'Brightness', 'Future school career'

Teachers' ratings and model at the end of the child's first year

We shall first look in Table 6.1 at the relationship between 'Brightness' and 'Future school career' to the general factor at time I and time II in both areas.

TABLE 6.1

General Factor	*Working class*		*Middle class*	
	Time I	*Time* II	*Time* I	*Time* II
Brightness	0·79	0·78	0·87	0·75
Future school career	0·80	0·80	0·83	0·82

We can see that this pair of ratings is very highly correlated with the general factor in both areas and at both times. Indeed, they represent the ratings which are the most important components of the teachers' model in both areas, and this component is a cognitive estimate of the child ('Brightness' and 'Future school career' are very highly inter-correlated).

The rating which has the lowest association with the general factor is 'Aggressiveness', as shown in Table 6.2.

Although the difference is not statistically significant, there is an indication that in the working-class area children rated as aggressive are very removed from the model of the successful pupil, whereas in the middle-class area such children are less removed from such a model. In other words, in the middle-class area the child who is

TABLE 6.2

General Factor	*Working class*		*Middle class*	
	Time I	*Time* II	*Time* I	*Time* II
Aggressiveness	0·23	0·16	0·53	0·33

rated as highly 'Aggressive' is relative to the working-class child judged more favourably. At time II, in *both* areas, the relationship between 'Aggressiveness' and the general factor is weaker, but it is still the case that in the middle-class area the correlation is still higher than in the working-class area, so that even at time II 'Aggressiveness' is viewed relatively more favourably in the middle-class area than in the working-class area. Clearly, we do not know what counts as aggressive behaviour for the teachers in the two areas. It may be that in the working-class area highly aggressive children may be more disruptive and more recalcitrant to control. It is possible that teachers in both areas share a common concept, but the incidence of such behaviour may be greater in one area than the other.

Let us now look at the relative position of 'Aggressiveness' and 'Independence'. We said earlier that these two ratings, in comparison with 'Co-operativeness' and 'Attentiveness', indicated more child-initiated behaviour than teacher-controlled or focused behaviour. We find that in both areas, at *time* I, 'Independence' is the rating which, apart from 'Aggressiveness', has the lowest correlation with the general factor (in passing we should note that in the working-class area this position is shared with 'Explanation'). However, the relationship of 'Aggressiveness' and 'Independence' to the general factor, at time I, is somewhat different in the two areas (see Table 6.3).

TABLE 6·3

General Factor	*Working class*	*Middle class*
	Time I	*Time* II
Aggressiveness	0·23	0·53
Independence	0·48	0·59

It would seem that in the teachers' model in the working-class area 'Aggressiveness' is clearly distinguished from 'Independence' in its contribution to the general factor; whereas in the middle-class area the contribution of 'Aggressiveness' and 'Independence' to the general factor are virtually identical. This would lead us to believe that in the middle-class area, at time I, we would expect, in general, that the teacher's model would place greater emphasis than in the working-class area on pupil-initiated behaviour. We should point out that 'place a greater emphasis' in the discussion means that pupil-initiated behaviour would be more closely related to the general factor. We can test this by examining those ratings which reflect pupil-initiated behaviour rather than teacher-controlled behaviour. Table 6.4 represents such ratings and their correlations with the general factor in the middle-class and working-class area at *time* I.

TABLE 6.4

	Working class	*Middle class*
Explanation	0·47	0·75*
Questioning	0·50	0·67
Aggressiveness	0·23	0·53
Independence	0·48	0·59

* statistical significant difference

There appears to be a trend in the *first* year that pupil-initiated behaviour, as indicated by the above ratings, is more highly related to the general factor in the middle-class area. It would seem that an active pupil role is more related to the model of the successful pupil in the middle-class area than in the working-class area.

Let us now look at 'Co-operativeness', 'Attentiveness' and 'Answering'. These three ratings are somewhat different from the above four in that they all refer to a large measure to teacher-controlled or focused behaviour. Table 6.5 shows their correlations with the general factor in the middle-class and working-class area at *time* I.

TABLE 6.5

	Working class	*Middle class*
Answering	0·73	0·74
Attentiveness	0·61	0·72
Co-operativeness	0·53	0·69

We can see that in both areas, at time I, teacher-controlled behaviour relates more strongly to the model of the successful pupil than does pupil-initiated behaviour, but in general there is *less* difference between these two in the *middle-class area*. In other words, the model of the successful pupil held by the teachers in the middle-class area stresses somewhat equally teacher-controlled behaviour and pupil-initiated behaviour; whereas in the working-class area there is an indication, but *only* an indication, that the emphasis falls somewhat heavier on teacher-controlled behaviour.

One result of grouping the correlations with the general factor in this way is that we may have missed an important finding. We will now look at the total array of correlations with the general factor in both areas at time I (see Table 6.6).

TABLE 6.6

	Expl.	*Quest.*	*Ans.*	*Aggr.*	*Ind.*	*Att.*	*Co-op.*	*Bri*	FSC
Working class	0·47	0·50	0·73*	0·23	0·48	0·61*	0·53	0·74	0·78
Middle class	0·75*	0·67	0·73	0·53	0·59	0·72	0·69	0·81	0·75

We can see by inspection that all the correlations with the general factor in the middle-class area bunch together rather more than do the correlations in the working-class area. If we leave on one side the ratings of 'Brightness' and 'Future school career' we can see that in the working-class area 'Answering' and 'Attentiveness' (the two starred correlations in the working-class array) stand out as the highest correlates of the general factor. The competence of answering fluently and the attitude of attentiveness are the most important components of the teachers' model of the successful infant-school child in the working-class area. And both 'Answering' and 'Attentiveness' belong to the cluster of teacher-controlled rather than pupil-initiated behaviour. If these are important ratings then the teachers will tend to select those pupils who display the behaviour associated with the ratings, and in this way a more passive relationship to the teachers is likely to be expected of the pupils. In the middle-class area, 'Explanation' (starred) correlates slightly more highly or about equally as highly with the general factor as 'Attentiveness' and 'Answering', with 'Questioning' and 'Co-operativeness' not far behind. Indeed, the correlation between '*Explanation*' and the general factor is the same as the correlation between 'Future school career' and the general factor (0·75). It is worthwhile pointing out again that the correlation between 'Explanation' and the general factor in the working-class area is 0·47. When we look at the middle-class array this confirms the earlier suggestion that *both* active and passive components of the teachers' model of the successful infant-school child are stressed in the middle-class area.

Before going on to examine in more detail the teachers' model at time II, it may be helpful to summarise the picture so far at time I.

1 In *both* areas the estimates of 'Brightness' and 'Future school career' correlate highest with the general factor, and 'Aggressiveness' shows the lowest correlation, but 'Aggressiveness' correlates more strongly with the general factor in the middle-class area.
2 In *both* areas the lowest correlations with the general factor are 'Aggressiveness' and 'Independence', but in the working-class area the correlation between 'Independence' and the general factor is *twice* the size of the correlation between 'Aggressiveness' and the general factor; whereas in the middle-class area there is little difference in the relative contribution of 'Aggressiveness' and 'Independence' to the general factor.
3 The correlations between pupil-initiated behaviour ('Explanation', 'Questioning', 'Aggressiveness', 'Independence') and the general factor, are all much *higher* in the *middle-class* area than in the working-class area.
4 In the middle-class area all correlations are relatively bunched together in their association with the general factor; whereas in the working-class area there is rather less bunching of the correlations.
5 In the working-class area 'Answering' and 'Attentiveness' stand out (among the ratings of specific behaviour) in their relation to the general factor; whereas it follows from 4 that this happens to a much *lesser* extent in the middle-class area.

In general, at time I, it appears that in the working-class area the crucial elements of the teachers' model consists of behaviour of the pupil which is highly teacher-controlled or teacher-focused; whereas pupil-initiated behaviour, 'Explanation', 'Questioning', 'Aggressiveness', 'Independence', is less crucial. Is this because in the working-class area pupil-initiated behaviour, the behaviour over which the pupil has more control, behaviour which is so to speak freely offered, is less acceptable because it is inappropriate to the teachers' model of the successful infant-school pupil? Is the working-class infant-school child less able to offer freely, on his accord, appropriate competencies and behaviours as judged by the teachers and, therefore, *has to learn what displays are good, acceptable or appropriate*? Is the working-class child's socialisation into the school by his family less able to equip him with favourable competencies, attitudes and work styles, so that his self-regulated behaviour is less acceptable to the teacher? The teachers' model, therefore, stresses control by the teacher. If this is so, then the working-class child's experience of school is essentially one of unlearning what he does naturally.

In the middle-class area, we find that *both* child-initiated and teacher-controlled behaviour are equally valued components of the teachers' model. Is this because there is greater fit between the socialisation of the middle-class child in his family and the various competencies, attitudes and work styles the teacher judges as acceptable? Much other research of the SRU on the children's families would suggest very strongly that this is indeed the case (see Appendix). As a result, what the middle-class child spontaneously offers is acceptable and valued by the teacher, and so it becomes an important index of the successful infant-school child. If this view is correct, then the working-class child has first to be socialised into the infant school before his own spontaneous behaviour is acceptable and appropriate. In the middle-class area the child already starts off with appropriate initial socialisation, and, therefore, we could expect in the second year that he be permitted greater discretion, and greater opportunity to be self-regulating.

The ratings and model at the end of the second year

We find at the end of the second year that in both areas the estimates of the child's 'Brightness' and 'Future school career', which were initially very high, have risen in both areas, to 0·80 and 0·80 in the working-class area and 0·83 and 0·82 in the middle-class area. Thus, these estimates which are highly correlated with the measured ability of the child at five years of age (see later discussion) improve their association with the general factor at the end of the second year. 'Aggressiveness', in both areas, is again the lowest correlate of the general factor, and in both areas the correlation is reduced (working-class time I, 0·23; time II, 0·16: middle-class time I, 0·59; time II, 0·33). It is still the case that 'Aggressiveness' correlates more highly with the general factor in the middle-class area. We find, however, that there have been some interesting changes in the association between the specific ratings and the general factor and, therefore, some changes in the model of the successful infant-school child held by the teachers.

The first thing to note is that all correlations with the general factor (with the exception of 'Aggressiveness') have risen.

'Answering', as in the first year, is still the highest correlation among the specific ratings with the general factor (0·79), and 'Independence', and 'Explanation' (0·57 and 0·06), are among the lowest with the exception of 'Aggressiveness'. Table 6.7 gives the correlations between all the ratings with the general factor at the end of the second year in the working-class area.

TABLE 6.7

General Factor	*Expl.*	*Quest.*	*Ans.*	*Aggr.*	*Ind.*	*Att.*	*Co-op.*	*Bri.*	FSC
Working class	0·57	0·63	0·78	0·16	0·60	0·63	0·64	0·80	0·80
Middle class	0·35	0·64	0·70	0·33	0·71	0·56	0·41	0·83	0·82

If we exclude 'Aggressiveness', the correlation between the specific ratings and the general factor in the working-class area now bunch together. This is a somewhat different picture than at the end of the first year where the bunching was somewhat weaker. Indeed, the array in the working-class area in the second year resembles the array in the middle-class area in the first year. The correlations between 'Explanation', 'Questioning', 'Independence', 'Co-operation' and the general factor have *all* risen. In other words, child-initiated behaviour is now relatively more emphasised in the teachers' model in the working-class area. It would appear that by the *second* year the behaviour the child is freely offering is now relatively more acceptable to the teacher, and, as a result, the correlations with the general factor are higher. This might indicate that, in the working-class area, the relative emphasis upon teacher control rather than child-initiated behaviour has socialised the children into the infant-school culture and, as a result, the children offer spontaneously behaviour that is more acceptable and appropriate. As a result, in the second year, child-initiated behaviour is relatively more highly correlated with the general factor. We would point out that, even in the second year, 'Answering' still stands out markedly among the specific ratings. 'Independence', however, has not changed its relative position from time I. These will be issues which we will be taking up later.

In the middle-class area, the picture, with the exception of the estimates of 'Brightness' and 'Future school career', has undergone a substantial change. 'Explanation' has dropped remarkably from 0·75 to 0·35, 'Independence' has risen from 0·59 to 0·71, 'Questioning' and 'Answering' have suffered only a slight downward change, 'Co-operativeness' has decreased sharply from 0·69 to 0·41, and 'Attentiveness' has dropped from 0·72 to 0·58. We now have a situation in the middle-class area where the two highest correlates with the general factor are 'Answering' (0·70) and 'Independence' (0·71), and 'Explanation' and 'Aggressiveness' are equally the two lowest, with 'Co-operativeness' not far behind (0.35, 0·33, 0·41). Indeed, the correlations in the middle-class area in the second year now bunch together far less and resemble somewhat the rating pattern in the working-class area in the *first* year. We would suggest that the changed picture in the middle-class area in the second year indicates that in the teachers' model of the successful infant-school child, 'Attentiveness', 'Co-operativeness' and 'Explanation' have reduced significance, but there has been an increase in the relevance of 'Independence'. In the second year the teacher is looking out for, noting favourably, the behaviour of the child, which counts for the teacher as indicating 'Independence', and this behaviour is of *equal* importance to 'Answering'.

We shall now undertake a more detailed analysis of the changes in size and position of the ratings in the two areas.

The most intriguing change in the middle-class area is the statistically significant reduction in the correlation between 'Explanation' and the general factor between time I and time II (from 0·75 to 0·35). 'Explanation' was the highest correlate among the specific ratings at time I, but at time II it is about the lowest. We decided, as one approach to this curious change, to examine the correlation between '*Explanation' at time* I and *all* first and second-year ratings in the middle-class and working-class area (see Table 6.8).

TABLE 6.8 *Pooled correlations between first-year 'Explanation' and all first- and second-year ratings in the working- and middle-class* LEAS

	Working-class LEA		*Middle-class* LEA	
	1st yr. rating	*2nd yr. rating*	*1st yr. rating*	*2nd yr. rating*
Explanation	1·000	0·482	1·000	0·360
Questioning	0·712	0·320	0·762	0·482
Answering	0·524	0·380	0·552	0·504
Aggressiveness	0·392	0·328	0·529	0·400
Independence	0·179	0·275	0·332	0·479
Attentiveness	0·089	−0·006	0·464	0·364
Co-operativeness	0·120	0·024	0·658	0·257
Brightness	0·266	0·180	0·521	0·561
Future school career	0·248	0·172	0·422	0·549

Normally we would expect a drop in these correlations between time I and time II because a different set of teachers are making judgments in the second year. We find, indeed, that this is the case in the *working-class area.* All correlations between 'Explanation' in the first year and *all* the ratings in the second year have dropped, with the exception of the correlation with 'Independence', which has risen from 0·18 to 0·28. However, in the middle-class area, we find that the correlations between 'Explanation' in the first year and 'Independence', 'Brightness' and 'Future school career' in the second year, have all *risen.* Indeed, 'Explanation' at time I has a much higher correlation with the above ratings (0·48, 0·56, 0·55) than it has with itself at time II (0·36).

We can see that at time I 'Explanation' correlates much more highly with *all* ratings in the middle-class area, than in the working-class area, and this is most marked for 'Aggressiveness' (0·53), 'Independence' (0·33), 'Attentiveness' (0·46), 'Co-operativeness' (0·66), 'Brightness' (0·56) and 'Future school career' (0·55). The respective correlations for the above ratings in the working-class area are 0·39, 0·18, 0·09, 0·12, 0·27 and 0·25. This difference in the size of the correlations with 'Explanation' is clearly reflected in the much higher correlation between 'Explanation' and the general factor at time I in the middle-class area. It is all the more remarkable that some of these initially much higher correlations between 'Explanation' and the ratings should have gone up in the second year when *a different set of teachers rated the children.* Clearly, this means that in the middle-class area, a child who initiates 'Explanation' frequently to the teacher not only is viewed as a successful infant-school child at time I, but is viewed as a *more* successful child at time II. *And this occurs when the contribution of 'Explanation' to the general factor has suffered a statistically significant drop at time* II.

The teachers' model of a successful infant-school child at time II in the middle-class area places a relatively *lower* emphasis upon the pupil coming up to the teacher and frequently offering explanations. Yet it is the case that 'Explanation' at time I has a higher correlation with 'Brightness' and 'Future school career' at time II than at time I. It may well be the case that the middle-class child who is rated highly on 'Explanation' in the first year, is also able to display those behaviours which call out a very favourable cognitive and educational judgment ('Brightness' and 'Future school career') on the part of teachers at the end of the second year.

Although 'Explanation' is of reduced relevance to the teacher in the middle-class area at time II, 'Independence' at time II is the highest correlate of the specific ratings with the general factor (0·71). It is also the case that 'Explanation' at time I correlates more highly with 'Independence' at time II than at time I (time I, 0·33; time II, 0·48). This would suggest that the middle-class child at time I, who is rated highly on 'Explanation', may also show signs of 'Independence', but this quality is of less significance to the teacher at time I, relative to the significance of 'Independence' at time II. In other words, the child, at time I, may be manifesting *both* behaviours, but 'Explanation' is of *greater* significance to the teacher; whereas at time II it is 'Independence' which is selected out and presumably reinforced. We can begin to see how the teacher selects out particular qualities of the pupil at different periods. It may be that the child has *not* changed, but the teacher's judgment of relevant qualities has changed. It is worth noting, in passing, that in the working-class area the *only* correlation between 'Explanation' in the first year and a rating in the second year which goes up, is the correlation with 'Independence' (time I, 0·20; time II, 0·28). However, we also know that 'Independence' is a *less* valued component of the teachers' model of the successful infant-school child in the working-class area at *both* time I and time II. Thus, in the working-class area, although there is some indication of an association between 'Explanation' in the first year, and 'Independence' in the second year, the quality of 'Independence' is less likely to be reinforced than the competency of 'Explanation'. We shall refer to this reversal later in the discussion.

The major points that emerge from this discussion is that different competencies and qualities are being picked out by the teacher at time I and time II. Thus, a child in the middle-class area, who is picked out because he possesses a quality highly favourable to the teachers' model in the first year, can apparently produce, in the second year, behaviour ('Independence') highly relevant to the teachers' model of a successful child when the initial quality, 'Explanation', is of *reduced* significance to the model. In the working-class area, although there is an increase in the association between 'Independence' and 'Explanation' at time II, the quality of 'Independence' is *less* relevant to the teachers' model and, therefore, presumably is not reinforced. Different attributes of the children are being selectively picked out, and presumably reinforced in the two areas. This process is at work from the first year in the infant school.

We now are in a position to consider in more detail changes in the attributes of the children in the two areas which are favourably judged by the teachers. We shall now be paying more attention to the increase and decrease in the size of the correlations between the ratings and general factor in both areas.

'Explanation', 'Questioning', 'Co-operativeness' and 'Attentiveness'

We shall focus on this quartet for two reasons. The first is that the analysis in Part I of this report shows that 'Explanation' and 'Questioning' form a distinct cluster, and so do 'Co-operativeness' and 'Attentiveness'. The second reason is that as we move from time I to time II the correlations between those ratings and the general factor go *up* in the working-class area, and go *down* in the middle-class area. Third, the first two ratings of 'Explanation' and 'Questioning' refer to child-initiated communications, whereas 'Co-operativeness' and 'Attentiveness' refer more to teacher-controlled or focused social behaviour.

At time I and time II there is a high correlation between 'Explanation' and 'Questioning' in both areas (average of 0·70). There is also a high correlation between 'Attentiveness' and 'Co-operativeness' in both areas, and at both times (average 0·65). This is, of course, what we should expect. What we shall do first is to take each area in turn and consider the inter-relationships *between* the two pairs of ratings.

In the working-class area, at time I, there are very weak correlations between 'Explanation' and 'Questioning', *and* 'Co-operativeness' and 'Attentiveness'. This means that pupil-initiated communication bears little relation to the teachers' judgment that the pupil's social relationship is appropriate. However, at the end of the second year there has been a dramatic *rise* in the correlations between 'Explanation' and 'Questioning', *and* 'Co-operativeness' and 'Attentiveness'. This is shown in Table 6.9.

Thus, at the end of the second year, in the working-class area, there is a significant relationship between the pupil who initiates communications of a linguistic-cognitive type *and* the pupil who displays an appropriate social relationship to the teacher. These two aspects of desirable pupil behaviour are now *more* related in the working-class area. Table 6.10 shows correlations for the middle-class area. In the middle-class area we can see that at time I there are high correlations between 'Explanation' and 'Co-operativeness' (0·66), 'Explanation' and 'Attentiveness' (0·46), 'Questioning' and 'Co-operativeness' (0·70), and 'Questioning' and 'Attentiveness' (0·45). The two aspects of desirable behaviour of the pupil (according to the teachers' model) are strongly associated in the middle-class area at the end of the *first* year at school. If the child is 'Co-operative' and 'Attentive', according to the teacher's judgment, then he is also very likely to initiate frequent communications to the teacher which

TABLE 6.9 *Correlations for the working-class area*

First school year

	Explanation	*Questioning*	*Co-operativeness*	*Attentive-ness*
Explanation	1·000			
Questioning	0·712	1·000		
Co-operativeness	0·120	0·188	1·000	
Attentiveness	0·089	0·152	0·773	1·000

Second school year

	Explanation	*Questioning*	*Co-operativeness*	*Attentive-ness*
Explanation	1·000			
Questioning	0·653	1·000		
Co-operativeness	0·367	0·392	1·000	
Attentiveness	0·265	0·324	0·741	1·000

involve spontaneous 'Questioning' *and* spontaneous 'Explanations'. However, at the end of the second year, the correlation between 'Explanation' and 'Co-operativeness' has dropped dramatically to 0·08, *and* the correlation between 'Explanation' and 'Attentiveness' has shown an equally sharp drop to 0·09. The correlation between 'Questioning' and 'Co-operativeness' has halved and is now 0·33. The correlation between 'Questioning' and 'Attentiveness' has suffered the least drop and is now 0·37 (a reduction of only 0·08). *Thus, whereas in the first year this quartet of correlations were strongly grouped together, by the end of the second year this quartet is only weakly related.* This is a very different picture from one we found in the working-class area. Indeed, it is almost a reversal of that situation. In the working-class area, in the first year, the quartet was very weakly associated, but at the end of the second year the quartet is very *strongly* associated. This picture of the reversed relationship between the two areas is one which somewhat resembles the picture we obtained when we compared the strength of the associations between individual ratings and the general factor at time I and time II. There we found that, in the working-class area, there was an *increase* in the correlations between the individual ratings (with the exception of 'Aggressiveness') and the general factor, whereas in the middle-class area, as we moved from time I to time II, there was a *drop* in the correlations between 'Explanation', 'Attentiveness', 'Co-operation' and, to a lesser extent, 'Questioning' and 'Answering', with the general factor. On the other hand, in the middle-class area there was a marked rise in the correlation between '*Independence*' and the general factor.

How do we account for the reversal in the correlations between members of this quartet between time I and time II in the two different areas? It appears to be the case that in the middle-class area at time II, because of the weak association between 'Co-operativeness' and 'Explanation' and 'Answering', a child who is rated highly on the *latter* pair need *not* be rated highly on the former rating. The extent to which the pupil 'Co-operates' with the teacher, and is 'Attentive', does not influence the judgment the teacher makes of the pupil who frequently and spontaneously offers 'Explanations' to the teacher. The teacher, then, in the middle-class area, distinguishes in his judgment between a cognitive quality of the child and the *social* quality of the relationship. Thus, 'Unco-operative' and less 'Attentive' pupils could still be rated high on 'Explanation'. In the same way, the strong relationship between 'Co-operativeness' and 'Questioning', which held at time I, is considerably reduced at time II; in fact, it is *halved.* We could now say that the *cognitive* quality of the pupil's relation to the teacher ('Questioning' and 'Explanation') is relatively only weakly related to the *social* quality of the relationship ('Co-operativeness'). Perhaps, the teachers in the middle-class area, in the second year, are looking out for a different type of social relationship between teacher and taught?

Now, we do have some evidence that this may well be the case.

TABLE 6.10 *Correlations for the middle-class area*

First school year

	Explanation	*Questioning*	*Co-operativeness*	*Attentiveness*
Explanation	1·000			
Questioning	0·762	1·000		
Co-operativeness	0·658	0·696	1·000	
Attentiveness	0·464	0·453	0·591	1·000

Second school year

	Explanation	*Questioning*	*Co-operativeness*	*Attentiveness*
Explanation	1·000			
Questioning	0·596	1·000		
Co-operativeness	0·079	0·332	1·000	
Attentiveness	0·086	0·366	0·686	1·000

We noted in the second year, in the middle-class area, that the correlation between 'Independence' and the general factor was the only rating of specific behaviour which *increased* in size. Indeed, excluding the estimates of 'Brightness' and 'Future school career', 'Independence' shares with 'Answering' the privilege of the rating which is the *highest* correlate of the general factor (0·71). 'Independence' has moved from one of the *lowest* correlates of the general factor at time I, to the *highest* correlate of the general factor at time II. It would seem, then, that it is plausible to argue that in the second year, in the middle-class area, the teacher is less concerned with the co-operating child, and more concerned to single out as especially desirable, especially relevant, to her model, the more self-regulating, autonomous, *independent* child. Whereas in the working-class area, although the correlation between 'Independence' and the general factor rises from 0·48 at time I to 0·60 at time II, the position of 'Independence' among the ratings of specific behaviours of the pupil is unchanged; it occupies the *fourth* position *at time* I *and time* II.

In the working-class area we can see that the increase in the strength of the relationship between 'Explanation' and 'Questioning', and 'Co-operativeness' and 'Attentiveness', from time I to time II, is paralleled by the increase in all correlations (except 'Aggressiveness') with the general factor at time II. Further, at time I, in the working-class area, the rating of 'Answering' is the rating of specific behaviour which has the highest correlation with the general factor (0·73). Whereas in the middle-class area it is '*Explanation*' which is the highest correlate of the general factor (0·75). It is also the case that, in the working-class area, 'Aggressiveness' at time I has a very weak relation to the general factor (0·23), whereas in the middle-class area at that period the correlation of 'Aggressiveness' with the general factor is 0·53. We might then argue that in the working-class area, at time I the crucial component of the teachers' model is whether the child *answers* the teacher fluently; whether the child is able to produce a fluent *reply* (fluency may, of course, be confounded with accuracy). In the middle-class area, however, '*Explanation*' is somewhat more highly correlated with the general factor than 'Answering' at time I. Indeed, 'Explanation' is the highest correlate of the specific ratings. Thus, in the working-class area the crucial judgment of the teacher refers to a teacher-controlled communication ('Answering'), whereas in the middle-class area the crucial judgment refers to *child*-initiated communication ('Explanation').

Further, at time I in the working-class area child-initiated communication ('Explanation' and 'Questioning') has little or no relationship with 'Co-operativeness' and 'Attentiveness', so that child-initiated cognitions are not related to the child expressing an appropriate relationship to the teacher. This may be because, for the working-class child, this is something *he has to learn*. However, the middle-class child has been socialised into the appropriate social relationship in his family, and therefore, at time I, the quartet of 'Explanation', 'Questioning', 'Co-operativeness' and 'Attentiveness' are all highly inter-correlated. In the working-class area, by time II, we find that the quartet are *more* closely related, so that the child-initiated cognitions ('Explanation' and 'Questioning') and appropriate social relationships are now linked. In other words, during the working-class child's two years in the infant school, he is being socialised into an appropriate relationship to the teacher. The latter involves the working-class child, relative to the middle-class child, in a position of doing what the teacher wants, learning the conduct that the teacher expects. *Child-initiated verbal cognitions are mediated through a social relationship in which the teacher's values and attitudes are dominant.*

In the middle-class area the child is already socialised into the appropriate social relationship, and, further, even in the first year, the teacher judges that *child*-initiated verbal cognitions are highly relevant to her model of the successful infant-school child. The teacher is also more accepting of the child's 'Aggressiveness'. At time I, in the middle-class area, because of the child's initial socialisation in his family, we have the close association of 'Co-operativeness', 'Attentiveness', 'Questioning' and 'Explanation', and these are *all* qualities which are highly relevant to the teachers' model of the successful infant-school pupil *in the first year*. At time II, we have seen that 'Independence' becomes an important component of the teachers' model in the middle-class area, and 'Co-operation' has *reduced* importance. Thus, in the second year, in the middle-class area, great significance is attached to the concept of the self-regulating, autonomous, independent child. (The 'Independence' dimension moves from *independence* at one extreme to *dependence* at the other.)

If this interpretation is correct, then we would expect a major weakening of the relationship between 'Co-operativeness' and 'Explanation'/'Questioning'. Child-initiated verbal cognitions are much less linked to 'Co-operativeness', because the relationship which the teacher judges to be important is '*Independence*'. The relationship between 'Questioning' and 'Co-operativeness', at time II in the middle-class area, has dropped, but it is still fairly strong (0·37). In general, then, in the middle-class area a high rating of child-initiated verbal cognitions is much less related to a teacher-controlled social relationship. If we wanted to state the comparison between the two areas in stark, simple terms, then we would say that in the middle-class area pupils are expected to be *self-regulating* whereas in the working-class area they are more *teacher-regulated. But the emphasis upon self-regulation / independence, in the middle-class area, is, itself, based upon an initial sharing between teacher and taught of the rules of appropriate conduct.*

Clearly, how the teacher rates various behaviours of the child in the classroom is, in part, a reflection of the curriculum and pedagogy. The teachers in the middle-class area in the second year seem to be working closely to the Plowden model, and this model affects the teacher's judgment *less* in the working-class area. In as much as the teachers' model affects the selective reinforcement of the behaviour of the child, then the middle-class infant-school child is being socialised into a more autonomous role where his spontaneous verbal cognitions are less controlled by the teacher, and this may well have important consequences for his later school career. This reflects and reinforces the focus of the socialisation of the middle-class child in his family. As other research of the SRU has shown (see Appendix; Bernstein and Henderson, 1969; Brandis and Henderson, 1970; Henderson, 1970; Jones, 1966), there is a continuity between the home and the school in the case of the middle-class child. In the case of the working-class child 'Independence' is much less stressed and teacher-regulated behaviour is more stressed. The teacher in the working-class area seems to be less able to take advantage of what the child *brings* to the school.

Conclusion

What we have done is to compare differences between the teachers' model of the successful infant-school child in a working-class area and a middle-class area. We started with a comparison between the individual ratings and general factor in the two areas. We noted how the contribution of the specific ratings to the general factor changed in the two areas between the end of the first year and the end of the second year. We developed in this discussion some ideas to account for the change. We then pursued these ideas in more detail by analysing major changes in the ratings. First, we noted the dramatic drop in the significance of 'Explanation' in the middle-class area at time II, and, second, we noted the reversal in the relationship between 'Explanation' and 'Questioning', *and* 'Co-operativeness' and 'Attentiveness'. The analysis gradually focused upon the relative significance of 'Independence' and child-initiated verbal cognitions in the middle-class area. We believe we have shown marked differences between the model of the successful infant-school child held by teachers in a middle-class area, and teachers in a working-class area. What we have as yet not commented on is the relationship between the estimates of 'Brightness' and the child's 'Future school career'. The reader will remember that the correlations between these ratings and the general factor was extremely high in both areas at time I, and the correlations increased in size in both areas at time II. We know that both these ratings correlate highly with the child's measured ability at five, but the size of this correlation varies with the area. In the next section of this report, we will be looking at the relation between the parents' social class, an Index of Communication and Control score, the sex of the child and his measured ability to the individual ratings and general factor.

Finally, there are a number of matters we should raise.

1 It is quite clear that we have no direct knowledge of what counts as a favourable or unfavourable judgment on any ratings, except in the case of the estimates of 'Brightness' and 'Future school career'. We do know that the variations between teachers is lowest for the ratings of 'Explanation', 'Answering', 'Questioning', 'Brightness' and 'Future school career' and significantly much higher for the ratings of the social relationship with the teacher ('Aggressiveness', 'Independence', 'Attentiveness' and 'Co-operativeness'). Thus, on the whole, the ratings which are most consistent between teachers are the speech ratings and the estimates of 'Brightness' and 'Future school career', whereas the ones which are less consistent are the ratings of social behaviour. On the other hand, the stability of the first factor (the general factor) is remarkably high in both areas. It is 0·68 in the working-class area, and 0·75 in the middle-class area. The criteria may change; but the overall value judgment remains extraordinarily stable.

2 It is also the case that we are concerned with thirty-four different teachers who vary in age, teaching experience and probably training. If these attributes of the teachers produced major differences in their rating behaviour, then we would not have such stability both within and between the first and second years. Indeed, what has to be explained is how thirty-four teachers in eighteen different schools can be so relatively homogeneous in their ratings; especially their ratings of the child's speech, brightness and academic prospects. On the other hand, each teacher is with her class continuously for a year, and for the greater part of each day, where she is able to view the same child across a range of activities. It is also the case that in the infant school there may be a more powerful and unifying ideology behind the teaching practice than at the secondary or even junior stage. Infant schools are relatively small, and staff are therefore

more likely to enter into closer relationships with each other than at the secondary and, possibly, junior stage. This would facilitate shared judgments within a school, but not necessarily between schools. However, this is not inevitably true, as in the middle-class area there are two schools with two teachers. In these schools the sample children were in two different classes. We know that there is considerable variation in one school on the relative contribution of 'Co-operativeness' and 'Aggressiveness' to the general factor in the second year, and considerable variation in the second school between the teachers in the strength of the relation between 'Co-operativeness' and 'Aggressiveness'.

3 Another factor which might affect the ratings is the material condition of the school. In general, the schools in the middle-class area are newer than the schools in the working-class area. However, there is only one post-war school in the middle-class area; there is one post-war school in the working-class area. There are two other schools in the working-class area which are relatively recent and spacious schools. It is also the case that at the time of the survey there were very few Commonwealth children in the schools.

4 We also should consider the pedagogy in the various schools. We did do some research upon the teaching practice in the various schools which included a full day's recording of the speech of the teacher. Unfortunately, this material is yet still to be analysed. It is our view that in general most schools were attempting some variation of child-regulated learning.

Chapter 7 The background variables and teachers' ratings

In this section we shall consider the relationships between the background variables and the teachers' ratings. The background variables are:

1 The sex of the child.
2 The IQ of the child.
3 Family social-class position.
4 An Index of Maternal Communication and Control.

We shall first discuss the relationships between each background variable and the general factor. We will then consider the relationships between the background variable and each individual rating. After we have completed these discussions we will evaluate the relative influence of each background variable upon the ratings.

The sex of the child

Sex and the general factor

In the middle-class area girls receive an overall more favourable rating than do boys. At time I the correlation between sex (girls) and the general factor is 0·33 and at time II the correlation is 0·29. However, in the working-class area at time I girls are *not* viewed more favourably than boys. By time II there is a small but significant correlation with the general factor of 0·19. In general girls are viewed more favourably than boys in the middle-class area.

Sex and the individual ratings

We shall now examine the relationships between the individual ratings and girls at time I and time II in each area.

In the working-class area at time I there are only two correlations with girls which are statistically significant. Girls are rated as less aggressive (−0·16) and less independent (−0·12). By the end of the second year girls are rated as significantly better than boys on 'Explanation' (0·16), 'Questioning' (0·16), 'Attentiveness' (0·20), 'Co-operativeness' (0·24) and 'Brightness' (0·13). We should point out that there is *no* significant difference between the measured intelligence of boys and girls. There is an interesting relationship between the teachers' ratings of the 'brightness' of girls, and the teachers' estimates of the 'Future school career' of girls. Although girls receive higher ratings of 'Brightness' than do boys, girls are not given a more favourable school prognosis than boys.

In the middle-class area at time I, with the exception of 'Independence', girls receive significantly more favourable ratings than boys. We can see from the array in Table 7.1 that teachers in the middle-class area, relative to the teachers in the working-class area, make a greater difference between boys and girls. By time II the general trend set out in Table 7.2 is a little different.

We can see that in general terms teachers in the working-class area, at time II, make more difference between the sexes, whereas in the middle-class area this difference is more marked at time I. It may well be that in the working-class area, at time I, the teachers are pre-occupied with a *general* problem of the socialisation of *children* into appropriate classroom behaviour because of the lack of adequate preparation in the family. By the end of the second year it may be that girls are producing behaviour more in accordance with the teacher's model. In other words, girls are responding more favourably than boys by the end of the second year. In this respect, it is of interest to note that the highest correlations in the working-class array at time II are with 'Attentiveness' (0·20) and 'Co-operativeness' (0·24). This would seem to indicate that girls are far less a control problem for the teachers and, perhaps because of this, are responding more favourably to the teaching with the consequence that they are rated brighter.

In the middle-class array the only correlation which has increased markedly in size between time I and time II is '*Independence*'. This contrast between 'Attentiveness' and 'Co-operativeness' in the working-class area, and 'Independence' in the middle-class area, brings out very sharply differences between the teachers' model in the two areas. The changes in the size of the correlation between sex and the individual ratings at time II in the middle-class area follow the changes in the size of the correlations with the general factor at time II. We noted in the previous chapter that at time II there was a marked drop in the correlation between 'Explanation' and the general factor, and we can see that this is reflected in the marked drop in the correlation with sex from 0·37 at time I to 0·03 at time II. In the same

TABLE 7.1

Time I

	Expl.	*Quest.*	*Ans.*	*Aggr.*	*Ind.*	*Att.*	*Co-op.*	*Bri.*	FSC
Working class	0·08	0·00	0·09	−0·16	−0·12	0·09	0·07	0·05	−0·02
Middle class	0·37	0·24	0·23	0·16	0·13	0·27	0·33	0·33	0·24

TABLE 7.2

Time II

	Expl.	*Quest.*	*Ans.*	*Aggr.*	*Ind.*	*Att.*	*Co-op.*	*Bri.*	FSC
Working class	0·16	0·16	0·06	−0·05	0·03	0·20	0·24	0·13	0·10
Middle class	0·03	0·15	0·14	−0·05	0·28	0·27	0·26	0·26	0·22

way, in the middle-class area, there was a marked rise in the correlation between 'Independence' and the general factor at time II, and we can see that there is, at time II, a corresponding rise in the correlation between sex and 'Independence'.

Despite the changes at time II in both areas, teachers in the middle-class area continue to make a greater difference between boys and girls (note the correlations in the middle-class area between sex and 'Independence', 'Brightness', 'Future school career' and 'Answering'. It also appears that girls are better able to meet the teachers' concept of 'Independence' than boys.) It is worthwhile anticipating our future discussion in order to sharpen our present-discussion of social class, sex and teachers' ratings. In the middle-class area, and only in the middle-class area, the correlation between sex and the general factor is as *high* as the correlation between the general factor and the scores on the Matrices, Crichton and EPVT. In other words, in the middle-class area the *sex* of the child (girl) exerts the *same* influence upon the teachers' overall rating as the child's measured ability. There is no question of the relatively greater fit, in the middle-class area, between the teachers' model of the successful infant-school child and girls. It is interesting to compare this fit with the middle-class mothers' reports that they are more coercive with their girls than with their boys (Bernstein and Brandis, 1970).

We have so far discussed differences in the way girls are evaluated by their teachers in the two areas. Now we shall look at some similarities. By time II girls in both areas are seen as much more attentive and co-operative than boys. Of greater interest is the trend in the relationship in both areas between 'Brightness' and 'Future school career'. Although girls in both areas are rated as brighter than boys, and are given a more favourable school prognosis, the correlations with 'Future school career' is lower than the correlation with 'Brightness'. We must hasten to add that this reduction in the size of the correlation with 'Future school career' is neither significant nor, indeed, very large. However, there is a sign of a possible trend which might become more pronounced as the children get older. If we are right then we have a situation where teachers have lower expectations of girls at the end of the first year of the infant school. From what we know of the effects of teachers' expectations it may be that girls, from their earliest days in school, are being socialised into lower educational achievement relative to the estimates of their 'Brightness'. Despite being viewed by the teacher as brighter than the boys, their school prognosis is relatively less favourable. We should emphasise again that this inference should be treated with caution because although the trend is consistent the drop in the correlation with 'Future school career' is indeed small.

Summary

In general we can say that the effect of the sex of the child upon the teachers' ratings is greater in the middle-class area than in the working-class area, although by time II there is a small but significant relation between sex and individual ratings and sex and the general factor in the working-class area. We have suggested that girls in the working-class area, rather than boys, are more able to attract favourable ratings. We have suggested that the more favourable ratings of girls, rather than boys, in the middle-class area may have some connection with the more restricted socialisation of the girl in the middle-class area. We must point out, however, that girls in the middle-class area, by the end of the second school year, are rated *more* independent than boys. It would appear that girls appear to adapt more to the teachers' requirements than do boys. It would be intriguing to speculate on the effect of more male teachers upon the children in the infant school. From the evidence presented here the infant-school environment favours girls. The differential *overall* rating of girls in the middle-class area is statistically significant beyond the 0·001 level at time I and time II; whereas the overall difference between boys and girls in the working-class area is not statistically significant at time I and is statistically significant at the much lower level of 0·05 at time II. Finally, the sex of the child in the middle-class area is as important as measured ability in its effect upon the overall teachers' rating.

The IQ of the child

Measured ability and the teachers' ratings

We will now consider the relationship between the child's measured ability and the teachers' ratings. After the children had been in the infant school for three weeks they were given three ability tests: the Raven's Progressive Matrices (children's version), the Crichton Vocabulary Scale and the English Version of the Peabody Vocabulary Scale (EPVT). The Matrices is a test of non-verbal ability, the Crichton is a test of active vocabulary, and the EPVT is a test of passive vocabulary.

Table 7.3 shows the correlations between the score on three tests and the general factor in both areas and at both times.

The first point we should like to make is that the correlation between measured ability and the general factor varies between 0·40 and 0·50 for the total sample. This is indeed a high correlation when one takes into account that the teachers never knew the IQ scores of the

TABLE 7.3

	Working class			*Middle class*		
	Matrices	EPVT	*Crichton*	*Matrices*	EPVT	*Crichton*
1st yr. ratings	0·38	0·41	0·52	0·29	0·30	0·38
2nd yr. ratings	0·44	0·40	0·53	0·28	0·25	0·30

children, and that the tests at five years of age are unreliable. The second general point is that the IQ measures are more highly correlated with the general factor at both times in the working-class area. We should, however, point out that the IQ variances in the working-class area are greater than the IQ variances in the middle-class area. This in itself would account for some of the difference in the size of the correlations. This difference in variance is, however, only significant for one test, the EPVT ($p < 0{\cdot}02$). This is of some interest because it is the EPVT which is most sensitive to environmental differences. It correlates with sex and ordinal position of the child (Bernstein and Brandis, 1970). In the middle-class area it correlates much higher with social class than the latter correlates with the other two tests (EPVT, 0·35; Matrices, 0·13; and Crichton, 0·23). It has the highest correlation with the Maternal Index of Communication and Control (EPVT, 0·27; Matrices, 0·13; Crichton, 0·10), even though the ICC's variance in the middle-class area is significantly smaller than in the working-class area.

Although difference in variance can account for part of the reduced correlation between IQ and ratings in the working-class area, it by no means accounts for *all* the difference. It is also the case that in the middle-class area the correlation between IQ and teachers' ratings actually *drops* at time II in the case of the EPVT and Crichton. The difference in the IQ correlations with the general factor in the two areas is not statistically significant, neither, of course, is the drop in the IQ correlations in the middle-class area. However, there appears to be a trend towards a *lower* correlation between IQ and the teachers' ratings in the middle-class area. We shall be returning to this point later in the discussion.

IQ and the individual ratings

On the whole, in both areas and at both times, the three IQ tests have much higher correlations with the ratings of 'Brightness' and 'Future school career'. (These two ratings are highly inter-correlated.) The matrix in Table 7.4 gives the pattern of correlations.

TABLE 7.4

		Middle class					Working class		
		Ma.	*Cr.*	EPVT			*Ma.*	*Cr.*	EPVT
Brightness	(1)	0·32	0·37	0·36	Brightness	(1)	0·35	0·45	0·43
Brightness	(2)	0·31	0·34	0·32	Brightness	(2)	0·42	0·46	0·43
Future school career	(1)	0·35	0·28	0·25	Future school career	(1)	0·40	0·44	0·46
Future school career	(2)	0·33	0·34	0·32	Future school career	(2)	0·44	0·51	0·45

We know also that the ratings in Table 7.4 are *exceptionally* highly correlated at both times and in both areas with the general factor. We now see that it is precisely these two ratings which correlate most highly with the children's measured ability.

We shall put together in one matrix the correlations between the general factor and the three IQ measures, and the correlations between these measures and 'Brightness' and 'Future school career' at time II (see Table 7.5).

TABLE 7.5

	Middle class				Working class		
	Ma.	*Cr.*	EPVT		*Ma.*	*Cr.*	EPVT
2nd yr. general factor	0·28	0·30	0·25	2nd yr. general factor	0·44	0·53	0·40
2nd yr. Future school career	0·33	0·34	0·32	2nd yr. Future school career	0·44	0·51	0·45
2nd yr. Brightness	0·31	0·34	0·32	2nd yr. Brightness	0·42	0·46	0·43

It is quite clear that in the infant schools in both areas the lower the IQ of the child, the less bright he is considered and the less favourable is his future school prognosis. We should point out that no school in either the middle-class or the working-class area was streamed. In as much as teachers have lower expectations of the less intelligent child (as measured by tests), then it is likely that such a child will fulfil the teachers' expectations; and this process is at work from the child's earliest days in the school. We have already noted a possibly stronger relation between IQ and a favourable teachers' rating in the working-class area.

TABLE 7.6

Working class	*Expl.*		*Quest.*		*Ans.*		*Aggr.*		*Ind.*		*Att.*		*Co-op.*	
	(1)	*(2)*	*(1)*	*(2)*	*(1)*	*(2)*	*(1)*	*(2)*	*(1)*	*(2)*	*(1)*	*(2)*	*(1)*	*(2)*
Matrices	0·09	0·15	0·17	0·23	0·33	0·40	0·00	0·08	0·23	0·23	0·34	0·42	0·29	0·33
Crichton	0·35	0·31	0·34	0·41	0·38	0·52	0·12	0·08	0·21	0·21	0·26	0·39	0·36	0·36
EPVT	0·17	0·18	0·28	0·22	0·32	0·39	0·00	0·01	0·14	0·15	0·38	0·42	0·26	0·32
Middle class														
Matrices	0·14	0·09	0·22	0·15	0·23	0·25	0·22	0·03	0·26	0·16	0·22	0·11	0·12	0·11
Crichton	0·24	0·11	0·29	0·29	0·30	0·23	0·10	0·08	0·16	0·12	0·42	0·13	0·23	0·13
EPVT	0·17	0·15	0·19	0·27	0·28	0·20	0·06	0·05	0·06	0·07	0·33	0·11	0·12	0·06

Levels of significance

Working-class area		Middle-class area	
$p < 0{\cdot}05$	$r > 0{\cdot}145$	$p < 0{\cdot}05$	$r > 0{\cdot}197$
$p < 0{\cdot}01$	$r > 0{\cdot}191$	$p < 0{\cdot}01$	$r > 0{\cdot}257$
$p < 0{\cdot}001$	$r > 0{\cdot}241$	$p < 0{\cdot}001$	$r > 0{\cdot}324$

We will look now at some of the relationships between individual ratings and IQ which appear to us to be worthy of comment. There is an overall trend for the correlation between all IQ measures and teacher ratings to go *up* in the working-class area, and on the whole to go *down* in the middle-class area (see Table 7.6).

On the whole it is the Crichton test, the test of active vocabulary, which has the highest correlations with the individual ratings. This finding holds for both areas. It is also the Crichton which shows the greatest drop in its correlation with the general factor between time I and time II in the middle-class area (see Table 7.7).

TABLE 7.7

	Working class *Crichton*	*Middle class* *Crichton*
1st yr. general factor	0·52	0·38
2nd yr. general factor	0·53	0·30

It is also the case that over one half of the IQ correlations with the ratings in the above arrays do not reach statistical significance in the *middle-class area.* We should bear in mind that the correlations in the working-class area are based upon a sample of 188, whereas the sample in the middle-class is only 99. The smaller the size of the sample the *higher* must be the correlation if it is to be statistically significant. One of the difficulties of interpreting this marked difference in the size of the correlations between the individual ratings and the IQ measures at time II in the two areas arises out of the reduced variance in the middle-class area. However, we are prepared to say at this point that the evidence suggests that in the working-class area, relative to the middle-class area, IQ is more strongly associated with favourable teachers' ratings.

This means that in the working-class area, if a child is not bright (as measured by IQ tests) when he *first* comes to school, then he is much less likely to receive favourable ratings from the teacher, compared with a less bright child in the middle-class area. That is, the teachers in the working-class area are screening the children in such a way that only the *initially* bright child conforms to the teacher's model. The correlations which show the greatest drop in their relation to IQ (and which are *consistent* across the three ability measures) are with 'Answering', 'Independence', 'Attentiveness' and 'Co-operativeness'. In the middle-class area for these ratings there is a consistent reduced correlation with the three IQ measures between time I and time II. We should also note that at time II the correlation in the working-class area between the Crichton and 'Explanation' is 0·31, whereas in the middle-class area the correlation is 0·11. We know that in the middle-class area the ratings of 'Attentiveness', 'Co-operativeness' and 'Explanation', have at time II a reduced significance for the teachers' model of the successful infant-school child; whereas 'Independence' at time II has more significance. Thus, in the middle-class area, we can see that the ratings which have *reduced* significance to the teachers' model have *reduced* IQ correlations. Further, the rating, 'Independence', which has increased significance for the teacher, has compared with the working-class area a *lower* correlation with IQ. The small increases in the correlations between 'Answering', 'Independence', 'Attentiveness' and 'Co-operativeness', and the three IQ measures in the working-class area, reflect the increase in the size of the correlations of these ratings with the general factor at time II.

We have focused our discussion upon the relatively weaker correlations between IQ and teachers' ratings at time II in the middle-class area. We have suggested that although IQ is relevant in both areas, it is less relevant in the middle-class area. If the process of screening the children in the middle-class area appears to be less based upon IQ, do other attributes of the children become more relevant in that area? In the working-class area we could argue that because the majority of the children are from the school's viewpoint ill-prepared the *majority* of the children are less able to offer behaviour which the teacher regards as appropriate. As a result the teachers in the first year do not even discriminate between the children in terms of their sex and only do so relatively weakly at the end of the second year. The major attribute of the children which is used as the basis for discrimination is their measured intelligence for it is this attribute which is more obviously and unevenly distributed among the children. However, once IQ becomes the criterion of discrimination then polarisation starts on that basis. We can expect that differences between the children based upon IQ will widen as the children get older so that eventually we reach a point where only 'bright' working-class children survive as successful pupils and the less 'bright' become progressively less successful.

All our evidence (see Appendix) points to the more appropriate preparation by the middle-class family of the child for school. Thus the majority of middle-class children offer behaviour which the teacher regards as appropriate. As a result appropriateness of these children's behaviour is *less* associated with their measured ability. Thus we would expect much weaker polarisation of the children in terms of their IQ with the result that more less 'bright' (as measured by tests) children in the middle class have a relatively better chance of becoming successful pupils. *And this process starts in the early days of the infant school.* It is a matter of interest that in the middle-class area the effect of the discrimination between boys and girls has as strong an effect upon the overall teachers' ratings (the general factor) as does the children's measured intelligence (see Table 7.8).

TABLE 7.8

		Middle class		
	Sex	*Matrices*	*Crichton*	EPVT
1st -yr. ratings	0·33	0·29	0·38	0·30
2nd-yr. ratings	0·29	0·28	0·30	0·25

It is possible that in the middle-class area the teachers' ratings are based upon a screening procedure which indicates that the teachers hold multiple criteria, whereas in the working-class area the screening procedure is simpler and is based upon IQ. This may explain why it is that the first factor in the working-class area explains *more* of the variance than it does in the middle-class area.

Summary

The IQ of the children is highly correlated with favourable teachers' ratings. There is a trend that IQ is more strongly associated with favourable ratings in the working-class area. 'Brightness' and 'Future school career' are the two ratings which have the highest correlations with the measures of IQ. We will be taking up this question again later in the report.

Social class and the teachers' ratings

Social class and the general factor

There are some initial issues which we must consider before commencing our discussion. The social-class variance is significantly greater in the middle-class area than in the working-class area (Brandis and Henderson, 1970). This means that the correlations with social class will be much higher in the middle-class area than in the working-class area. However, because the school class is the unit for analysis, and because the social composition of each school class is relatively homogeneous, the correlations with social class should be overall small. This turns out to be the case. Social class has the weakest relationship with the general factor than any of the other background variables: IQ, sex, ICC. However, it is higher in the working-class than in the middle-class area, and this difference is particularly marked at time II (see Table 7.9).

TABLE 7.9

	Working class Social class	*Middle class Social class*
1st-yr. general factor	0·26	0·18
2nd-yr. general factor	0·26	0·09

Thus, despite the *reduced* social-class variance and the greater size of the working-class sample, there is a stronger association between social class and the overall teachers' ratings (the general factor) in the working-class area. We can say that relative to the working-class area the class background of the child *and* his measured ability is of less relevance to the teachers' model in the middle-class area.

Social class and the individual ratings

We shall now turn to the social-class associations with the individual ratings. We should expect findings similar to the above. This is indeed necessarily the case. The class correlations with the rating is higher (with the exception of 'Aggressiveness') in the working-class area at both times. There is virtually no correlation between class and 'Aggressiveness' in the working-class area, presumably because of the reduced variance of that rating. In the middle-class area the correlation is −0·14 (not significant) at time I and −0·23 (significant) at time II. At time II the latter correlation is the highest in the middle-class array. Thus, within the middle-class area the *lower* the social class the more likely that the child is seen as 'aggressive'. It is possible that 'aggressive' children might stand out more in the middle-class area. There are three negative correlations with social class in the middle-class, none of which are significant at time I: 'Explanation' (−0·11), 'Questioning' (−0·04) and 'Aggressiveness' (−0·14). At time II these are reduced to two: 'Questioning' (−0·03) 'Aggressiveness' (−0·23). There is a small suggestion that the 'active' child may come from a lower social class in the middle-class area. In the working-class area there is a small rise in the social-class correlations with 'Answering', 'Independence', 'Co-operativeness', 'Brightness' and 'Future school career', between time I and time II, and a small reduction in the social-class correlations with 'Explanation', 'Questioning', 'Aggressiveness' and 'Attentiveness'. These changes are quite small and only the class correlation with '*Attentiveness*' is significant.

Summary

In general social class is, relative to the other background variables, only weakly related to the teachers' ratings, although, on the whole, the relationship with social class is stronger in the working-class area. The sex of the child in the middle-class area bears a stronger relation to the teachers' ratings than does the child's family class position.

Index of Communication and Control

Index of Communication and Control and the teachers' ratings

As the Maternal Index of Communication and Control is discussed at length in Brandis and Henderson, 1970, we shall mention only briefly its components. The ICC was constructed out of the following elements:

1 The extent to which the mother reported that she would not avoid or evade answering difficult questions which her child might put.
2 The extent to which the mother accepted child-initiated talk.
3 The frequency with which the mother said she used physical punishment.
4 The frequency with which the mother said she would use child-oriented appeals of a cognitive type when her child misbehaved.
5 The stress the mother placed upon the exploratory function of toys.

Thus, if a mother received a high ICC score she reported that she talked to the child frequently, answered difficult questions, rarely physically punished the child, used appeals which related the consequence of the child's action to the child and stressed the exploratory function of toys. The ICC was constructed out of data we obtained when we interviewed the mother approximately four months *before* her child went to school for the first time. We have found on a number of occasions that ICC discriminates *within* social class in the working-class area (Bernstein and Young, 1967; Bernstein and Brandis, 1970). However, as we expected, it has very little discrimination in the middle-class area. This is a result of the statistically significant reduced variance in the middle-class area.

Index of Communication and Control and the general factor

We shall again look first at the overall picture. With the exception of the Matrices, the correlations between ICC and the IQ measures are higher with the ICC than with social class in the working-class area. In the middle-class area only the correlation between the EPVT and the ICC is statistically significant (0·24) and here the social-class correlation is higher (0·35). We shall now present the total matrix of correlation between all the background variables and the general factor at time I and time II (Table 7.10).

We can see that in the working-class area the correlation between the ICC and the general factor at time I and time II is the second highest of the background variables, and it closely follows the correlations between the IQ measures and the general factor (with the exception of the Crichton). It is a matter of interest that the ICC has the highest correlation with the Crichton. Further, in the working-class area the rise in the ICC's correlation with the first- and second-year ratings (from 0·35 to 0·43) is *greater* than the changes in the size of the correlation with any of the IQ measures. Thus there is a hint that the ICC score obtained *before* the child went to school may have an increased relation to teachers' ratings as the children get older. *In other words the effect of the communication structure in the working-class families may increase as the child gets older.*

In the middle-class area we can see that there is no relation between the ICC score and the general factor; indeed, at time II it becomes very slightly negative. This is exactly what we expected (Brandis and Bernstein, 1970; Bernstein and Young, 1966) for there is markedly less variation in ICC scores in the middle-class area. We can see that the correlation between sex and the ICC score in the middle-class area is negative and statistically significant (—0·24). This indicates that girls in the middle-class area are brought up in a more restrictive fashion than boys. (See earlier discussion of the relationship between sex and the teachers' ratings in the middle-class area.)

Index of Communication and Control and the individual ratings

We shall now turn to the relationship between the individual ratings and the ICC at time I and time II in both areas. We shall start with the middle-class area (see Table 7.11) because, as the above matrix indicates, we shall find little to discuss. The only correlation which is statistically significant at time I is the correlation of 0·24 between

TABLE 7.10 *Pooled correlations between six independent variables and first- and second-year first rating-factors*

(i) Working-class LEA

		Home background			IQ *test scores*		*First rating-factor*	
	Sex	*Soc. class*	ICC	*Matrices*	EPVT	*Crichton*	*1st-yr.*	*2nd-yr.*
Sex	1·000							
Social class	−0·090	1·000						
ICC	−0·016	0·400	1·000					
Matrices	−0·084	0·189	0·150	1·000				
EPVT	−0·079	0·229	0·250	0·383	1·000			
Crichton	0·056	0·213	0·271	0·351	0·558	1·000		
1st-yr. rating	0·066	0·261	0·351	0·381	0·407	0·517	1·000	
2nd-yr. rating	0·166	0·255	0·426	0·436	0·396	0·527	0·675	1·000

(ii) Middle-class LEA

		Home background			IQ *test scores*		*First rating-factor*	
	Sex	*Soc. class*	ICC	*Matrices*	EPVT	*Crichton*	*1st yr.*	*2nd yr.*
Sex	1·000							
Social class	−0·027	1·000						
ICC	−0·236	0·229	1·000					
Matrices	−0·023	0·133	0·126	1·000				
EPVT	0·005	0·345	0·285	0·180	1·000			
Crichton	−0·017	0·225	0·100	0·121	0·640	1·000		
1st-yr. rating	0·331	0·181	0·028	0·285	0·297	0·380	1·000	
2nd-yr. rating	0·293	0·089	−0·042	0·283	0·249	0·296	0·749	1·000

NOTE (a) ICC sample is reduced by 3 schools, 69 children in the working-class LEA, and by 3 children in the middle-class LEA. If the ICC sample is taken in the working-class LEA, all correlations between independent variables and ratings go up.

(b) Sex is scored so that female is equivalent to a 'high' score.

TABLE 7.11

Middle-class area						
Time I	*Sex*	*Social class*	*Matrices*	*Crichton*	EPVT	ICC
Exp.	0·365	−0·114	0·142	0·243	0·173	−0·064
Ques.	0·237	−0·040	0·223	0·290	0·193	−0·032
Ans.	0·232	0·133	0·233	0·300	0·287	0·081
Agg.	0·156	−0·143	0·216	0·100	0·059	0·054
Ind.	0·113	0·076	0·255	0·158	0·058	0·244
Att.	0·266	0·249	0·215	0·420	0·332	−0·095
Co-op.	0·326	0·079	0·121	0·229	0·120	−0·069
Bri.	0·327	0·198	0·322	0·368	0·356	−0·024
FSC.	0·240	0·280	0·345	0·287	0·248	0·020
Time II						
Exp.	0·034	0·006	0·086	0·108	0·115	0·065
Ques.	0·146	−0·029	0·146	0·290	0·273	−0·072
Ans.	0·144	0·094	0·246	0·231	0·203	−0·006
Agg.	−0·051	−0·231	0·033	0·087	0·049	0·126
Ind.	0·277	0·014	0·156	0·117	0·074	0·093
Att.	0·267	0·139	0·234	0·190	0·107	−0·112
Co-op.	0·257	0·116	0·114	0·131	0·060	−0·156
Bri.	0·258	0·156	0·312	0·344	0·315	−0·023
FSC.	0·221	0·172	0·329	0·336	0·321	0·029

the ICC and 'Independence'. Perhaps, because of this, we find that there are five correlations which are extremely small but *all* negative: 'Explanation', 'Questioning', 'Attentiveness', 'Co-operativeness' and 'Brightness'. In the second year the only correlation which is statistically significant is the correlation between the ICC and 'Co-operativeness', which is negative (−0·16). In the second year we also find five negative correlations with the ICC: 'Questioning', −0·07; 'Answering', −0·01; 'Attentiveness', −0·11; 'Co-operativeness', −0·16; 'Brightness', −0·02. The correlation with 'Aggressiveness' is 0·13, which just fails to be significant at the 0·05 level. There is then a hint that children in the middle-class area whose mothers have *high* index scores are possibly a little likely to be seen somewhat *unfavourably* by the teacher. Perhaps these children do not take kindly to the teachers' concept of appropriate classroom behaviour.

As there is a correlation between social class and the ICC scores (0·23), this would indicate that such children come from high social-class families with high ICC scores *and* they are boys who are likely to be of high measured intelligence.

In the working-class area, as we expect, the correlations between the ICC scores and the individual ratings at time I and time II are much higher than in the middle-class area (see Table 7.12). At both times the highest correlations with the ICC are with 'Brightness' and 'Future school career'. Indeed, at time I the correlations between the ICC and the above ratings are on the whole *higher* than the correlations between the IQ measures and these two ratings. At time I the next highest correlations between the ICC and the individual ratings are with 'Answering' (0·21) and 'Attentiveness' (0·34). (All correlations between the ICC and the ratings, except for 'Aggressiveness', are statistically significant at time I and time II.) It would seem that in the working-class area families with high ICC scores have children who are viewed (relative to the other specific ratings) as being particularly fluent in answering questions and who are highly attentive. At time II there is a rise in the correlations with 'Explanation', 'Questioning', 'Answering' and 'Co-operativeness'. This rise is

TABLE 7.12

Working-class area

Time I	*Sex*	*Social class*	*Matrices*	*Crichton*	EPVT	ICC*
Exp.	0·082	0·160	0·088	0·349	0·172	0·159
Ques.	0·004	0·154	0·174	0·342	0·278	0·140
Ans.	0·085	0·204	0·330	0·378	0·320	0·213
Agg.	−0·160	−0·045	0·002	0·115	−0·003	−0·022
Ind.	−0·123	0·128	0·231	0·211	0·138	0·155
Att.	0·093	0·255	0·335	0·392	0·328	0·335
Co-op.	0·072	0·154	0·288	0·361	0·263	0·164
Bri.	0·050	0·246	0·346	0·453	0·385	0·432
FSC.	−0·019	0·274	0·400	0·443	0·420	0·455
Time II						
Exp.	0·156	0·105	0·149	0·307	0·157	0·160
Ques.	0·164	0·099	0·227	0·406	0·221	0·338
Ans.	0·059	0·243	0·397	0·515	0·387	0·418
Agg.	−0·045	0·005	−0·061	0·076	−0·010	0·062
Ind.	0·032	0·185	0·233	0·258	0·146	0·152
Att.	0·203	0·180	0·420	0·404	0·422	0·266
Co-op.	0·241	0·187	0·327	0·356	0·322	0·338
Bri.	0·130	0·325	0·420	0·463	0·415	0·432
FSC.	0·102	0·302	0·444	0·508	0·485	0·451

* It must be borne in mind that the ICC sample is smaller than the IQ sample. It is unlikely that the correlation with the ICC would show a different pattern with an increased sample size.

especially marked for 'Questioning' (time I, $r = 0{\cdot}14$; time II, $r = 0{\cdot}39$), 'Answering' (time I, $r = 0{\cdot}21$; time II, $r = 0{\cdot}42$) and 'Co-operativeness' (time I, $r = 0{\cdot}16$; time II, $r = 0{\cdot}34$). Indeed, in the case of these three ratings, the correlations with the ICC are higher than with the IQ measures, with the exception of the Crichton.

These correlations with the Maternal Index of Communication and Control (especially at time II) indicate the validity of this measure. It was based on data obtained from the mothers of the children over two years earlier than the second teachers' ratings. It was considered to represent the frequency, quality and range of the *mother's reported* communication to her child.

We now find that ICC has relatively strong correlation (indeed often stronger than the IQ measures) with the individual teachers' ratings at the end of the children's second year at school. The Index correlates well with the teachers' assessment of appropriate speech behaviour of the children and with the teachers' assessment of what she considers is an appropriate social relationship to her. We should also bear in mind that mothers who have high scores on ICC see their relationship to the school as one of co-operation. Such mothers also believe that there will be few disagreements between the home and the school (Bernstein and Brandis, 1970).

There is a possibility that high ICC scores call out somewhat different judgments from the teachers in the working-class area than from the teachers in the middle-class area. We noticed that there were five negative correlations with the ICC at time I and five negative correlations at time II in the middle-class area. It is also the case that in the middle-class area there is a positive correlation between the ICC and 'Aggressiveness' (0·13). In the working-class area, however, there is only one negative correlation with the ICC, 'Aggressiveness' (—0·01). There is then a hint that in the middle-class area, children whose mothers attain high ICC scores are somewhat *less* favourably judged by the teacher; whereas in the working-class area they are *much* more favourably judged. (We should, however, note that in the working-class area the only correlation with the ICC, which drops at time II, is the correlation with 'Attentiveness' (time I, $r = 0{\cdot}34$; time II, $r = 0{\cdot}27$).) This suggests that high ICC scores in the working-class area do not mean the same thing as high ICC scores in the middle-class area. *It is not necessarily the case that mothers with high ICC scores in the working-class area are middle-class in their orientation.*

Summary

In general, the Maternal Index of Communication and Control is relatively strongly correlated in the working-class area with children who receive favourable teachers' ratings. Its influence in the working-class area *increases* with time and this is particularly true in the case of the teachers' ratings of the child's speech behaviour and aspects of the child's social relationship to the teacher. *The influence of the ICC on the teachers' ratings is greater than the family's social-class position, the sex of the child, and greater than the child's measured ability, with the exception of the Crichton.* There is also an indication that high ICC scores in the working-class area have a different effect upon the teachers' ratings in the working-class area than in the middle-class area.

The background variables and the teachers' ratings

We shall now consider the relative effects of the various background variables upon the teachers' ratings. We shall first consider these effects in terms of the *total* sample. We shall sum the general factor at time I and time II. Table 7.13 sets out the correlations between the summed general factors and the *total* sample.

TABLE 7.13

	Sex	*Social class*	*Matrices*	*Crichton*	EPVT	ICC
First factors	0·20	0·23	0·40	0·50	0·40	0·24

Thus, if we take the *total* sample, then by far the strongest influence upon the teachers' ratings is measured ability, followed by the ICC, then social class, and finally sex. However, such a picture is misleading, for when we considered each area in turn we saw that different background variables have different influences in the two areas. In the middle-class area, compared with the working-class area, social class has little effect; the ICC has even less; IQ, although important, has a relatively reduced influence; whereas the influence of sex is almost as strong as IQ. In the working-class area the relationship between the general factor and the background variables is such that by time II the ICC shares with IQ the privilege of having the greatest influence, although the *Crichton* test has a greater influence than the ICC. Social class comes next, and sex is only weakly related to the second-year ratings. Thus, in the middle-class area, only *sex* and *IQ* have a strong relationship with the ratings, and there is some indication that the effect of IQ is weakening slightly by the end of the second year. This weakening is most pronounced in the case of the Crichton, although that particular test emerged as the best predictor in both areas.

A similar picture emerged when we examined the correlation between each background variable and the individual ratings. It would seem that because sex and IQ are the only background variables which have a significant effect upon the teachers' ratings, the middle-class is more homogeneous in its socialisation of the child into the infant school. Whereas in the working-class there is much greater variation in such socialisation practices, and, as a result, all the background variables, with the exception of sex, have an influence upon the teachers' ratings. It would seem that of these background variables, with the exception of the Crichton, the most important influence appears to be the communication structure in the family.

Social class, ICC and IQ in the working-class area

We shall now examine more closely the relationship between social class, the ICC and the IQ measures in the *working-class area*. The correlation between social class and the ICC is 0·40. Thus, the higher the social class of the family, the higher the ICC scores. With the exception of the Matrices (the test of non-verbal IQ), the IQ correlations with the ICC are higher than the correlations between social class and the IQ measures, and this is relatively more marked for the Crichton (social class, $r = 0{\cdot}21$; ICC, $r = 0{\cdot}27$). We have also shown that when the ICC is correlated with a more reliable IQ test, the WISC, it yields a correlation of 0·38 with a sample of 162 working-class children (Brandis and Bernstein, 1970). As we have no IQ measures of the parents we are in no position to indicate a causal relationship between the ICC and IQ scores. Partialling procedures do not really help, for if we take teachers' ratings, ICC and IQ, whichever of the latter pair we partial out there will always be a significant residual. However, it is unlikely that high ICC scores depress IQ, whereas it is more likely that low ICC scores depress IQ. Whatever the potential of the child the ICC score presumably acts to facilitate or reduce the full expression of this potential; but also, more importantly, it *focuses* it. We should regard the ICC score as representing a facilitating and focusing process. We could now formulate the relationships between social class, ICC and IQ in the following way. Social class represents objective relationships; their subject significance is mediated through the communication structure within the family, which in turn facilitates and *focuses* the child's potential, which in turn becomes a crucial influence upon the teachers' ratings in the working-class area. This formulation leads us on to our final discussion of the relationships between teachers' ratings, IQ and social class (see Table 7.14).

TABLE 7.14 *Pooled correlations between two verbal* IQ *tests, two non-verbal* IQ *tests, and two teachers' ratings (first factors) for each* LEA

Working-class LEA (n = 182)	*Non-verbal* IQ		*Verbal* IQ		*First rating-factor*	
	Matrices	WISC	*Crichton*	WISC	*1st yr.*	*2nd yr.*
Matrices	1·000					
WISC non-verbal	0·560	1·000				
Crichton	0·342	0·368	1·000			
WISC verbal	0·324	0·397	0·627	1·000		
1st yr. rating	0·384	0·440	0·522	0·483	1·000	
2nd yr. rating	0·438	0·438	0·532	0·476	0·674	1·000
Middle-class LEA (n = 99)	*Non-verbal* IQ		*Verbal* IQ		*First rating-factor*	
	Matrices	WISC	*Crichton*	WISC	*1st yr.*	*2nd yr.*
Matrices	1·000					
WISC non-verbal	0·351	1·000				
Crichton	0·121	0·164	1·000			
WISC verbal	0·127	0·150	0·483	1·000		
1st yr. rating	0·285	0·151	0·380	0·350	1·000	
2nd yr. rating	0·283	0·129	0·296	0·431	0·749	1·000

Teachers' ratings, IQ and social class

In order to explore these inter-relationships in more detail, we added to our original matrix of IQ measures the WISC scores of the children which we obtained at the beginning of their second year in the infant school when they were six years of age. For reasons of economy, only the short form of the WISC (two performances and two verbal tests) was given to the children in the middle-class area; in the working-class area the full-scale of the WISC was given to the children. For the purpose of comparison between the areas we used only the shortened form of the WISC in the working-class area. (The correlation between the short form and the full-scale version of the WISC is 0·90.) Despite this high inter-correlation, we should bear in mind that in the middle-class area the children received only four tests, so that they did not have the warm-up opportunity available to the working-class children where the four sub-test scores were abstracted from the full range of tests which makes up the full-scale version.

We give now the correlation matrix containing all the IQ measures and the general factor at time I and time II. We can see from the matrix that in the working-class area the correlation between the performance (non-verbal) scales of the WISC and the verbal scales is 0·40; whereas in the middle-class area the correlation between the performance and verbal scales is 0·15. We should remember that the size of the sample in the working-class area is 182 and the sample size in the middle-class area is 99. Now, when we examine the correlation between the Matrices and the Crichton, we find in the working-class area that it is higher (0·34) than the correlation in the middle-class area between these two tests (0·12). In other words, there is a much closer relationship between verbal and non-verbal scores in the *working-class* than there is in the middle-class area. It seems that at ages five and six years the verbal and non-verbal competences of the middle-class children are more differentiated than in the working-class area. In the working-class area these competencies are much less differentiated. This finding calls to mind the work of Mitchell (1956), who compared the factorial organisation of mental abilities for well-defined high- and low-status groups. He found that the organisation of mental abilities was much less differentiated for the low-status groups.

Now, when we examine the relationship between all the IQ tests and the teachers' ratings, the findings are as shown in Table 7.15.

TABLE 7.15

Working class	*Matrices*	WISC *(performance)*	*Crichton*	WISC *(verbal)*	EPVT
1st-yr. ratings	0·38	0·38	0·52	0·48	0·41
2nd-yr. ratings	0·44	0·44	0·53	0·48	0·40
Middle class					
1st-yr. ratings	0·29	0·15	0·38	0·35	0·38
2nd-yr. ratings	0·28	0·13	0·30	0·43	0·30

We shall first comment on the EPVT. This test is carried out in a situation which is similar to the two non-verbal (performance) tests. There is little verbal interaction between tester and child. All that is required of the child is for him to point to one out of four pictures which represent an object or person verbally mentioned by the tester. It is essentially a test of passive vocabulary. When we consider the correlations of this test, we find:

1 At time I in the working-class area, the size of the EPVT correlations with the general factor is more like the Matrices and

WISC performance than it is like the Crichton and WISC verbal correlations with the general factor.

2 In the middle-class area, on the other hand, the EPVT yields correlations more similar to the two other tests.

Thus, there is some indication that the EPVT in the working-class area behaves rather like the performance tests.

We are left with the curious behaviour of the WISC in the middle-class area. If we exclude the WISC performance scale at time I, then all tests share similar correlations with the general factor. At time II, because of the downward movements of the Crichton and EPVT and an upward movement of the WISC verbal, the WISC as a whole stands out from the array. Thus, at time II in the middle-class area, the WISC performance has the lowest and the WISC verbal the highest correlation with the general factor. It is also the case that the inter-correlations between the Matrices and the Crichton are equally as low as the inter-correlations between the WISC verbal and performance. We can conclude from this that in the middle-class area, and only in the middle-class area, the competencies underlying the WISC performance have the least relevance to the teachers' model, whereas the competencies underlying the WISC verbal have the greatest relevance to the teachers' model. In other words, the WISC performance test in the *middle-class area* bears very little relation to the child's competencies and forms of social relation which the teacher evaluates favourably.

Let us see what *might* lie behind this conclusion. The competencies measured by the short form of the WISC performance are essentially spatial-perceptual (block design, object assembly), whereas the competencies measured by the Matrices entail a more pronounced cognitive element (the ability to discover the logical structure of a pattern). We could argue that, because of this difference in the underlying competencies, we could expect that the Matrices has a more direct bearing on the educational context than the WISC performance, and therefore the correlation between the Matrices and the general factor is much higher. When we look at the verbal tests, the major difference between the WISC verbal and the other two tests is that the WISC verbal contains a similarity scale. This scale is concerned to test analogic thinking (how are two things alike?). The WISC vocabulary scale is similar to the vocabulary scale of the Crichton. This verbal analogic competence may be of more relevance in the middle-class area than the children's competence in vocabulary. Thus, the correlation at the end of the second year between the WISC verbal and the general factor rises and it is the *only* correlation to rise. The WISC at time II in the middle-class area measures competences which are most and least relevant to the competencies valued by the teachers. The Crichton and EPVT measure competencies which are of reduced relevance, i.e. vocabulary definition, and so we find a reduction in their correlations with the general factor. We are arguing that the teachers in the middle-class area are basing their judgment more upon *analogical* reasoning. It is a matter of interest that in the second year, in the middle-class area, '*Independence*' is the attribute of the pupil which increases *most* markedly in its relevance for the teacher.

In the working-class area, it is the Crichton at time I and time II which has the highest correlation with the general factor, and the Crichton is a test of active *vocabulary*. Of the three verbal tests, it is the Crichton which produces the largest difference *between* the areas in the size of the correlation with the general factor. Thus, at time II it is the competence of active word definition which is most valued in the working-class area, and (taking the Crichton as criterion) *least* valued in the middle-class area. We know further that there is a sharp drop in the teachers' evaluation of 'Explanation' in the middle-class area by the end of the second year. We are suggesting that in the working-class area the teachers are distinguishing between the children in the verbal area in terms of their ability to use words actively and with discrimination, whereas in the middle-class area, although the verbal area is relevant, the teachers are more concerned with verbal analogic reasoning. From another point of view, the teachers in the working-class area are looking out for *any* index of 'Brightness', and as a consequence we have higher correlations with non-verbal tests. In other words, the teachers in the working-class areas have a less *selective* concept of 'Brightness' for *they* may consider that this attribute is in short supply in a working-class area. In the middle-class area this attribute is less in short supply and, as a consequence, the teachers' concept is more *selective*. It would follow that a particular type of ability is being fostered by teachers in the middle-class areas: verbal analogic reasoning.

We thus obtain the greatest difference *between* the two areas in the correlation between the general factor and the Crichton *and* the two non-verbal tests. We have seen as a corollary that the *less* culturally-biased tests (the non-verbal tests) are *much more relevant in the working-class area.* The polarisation of the children in the working-class area is based far more upon measures of intelligence than it is in the middle-class area. There is also a distinct possibility that the teachers in the middle-class area are selecting out *verbal analogic reasoning* as a cognitive attribute of especial significance, and presumably they will attempt to foster its development. We have also presented evidence which suggests that the communication structure in the middle-class family is more selective and focused than in the working-class family, in terms of its relationship to what counts as educationally relevant abilities and competencies. We argued that this gives rise to a greater differentiation of competences in the child, with the consequence that there are relatively weaker correlations between verbal and performance tests. The teacher in turn responds less to vocabulary and performance skills (especially those measured by the WISC), and more to verbal analogic skills. The differentiation of the middle-class child's abilities and competences is further selectively focused by the teacher who appears to judge most favourably independence and verbal analogic skills. In as much as the teacher recognises and evaluates these very positively, then presumably she will be interested in their development. The middle-class child is being *directed towards generic principles to be realised by himself.*

In order to test the above inferences, we shall now examine the pattern of correlations between the similarity scale and the vocabulary scale of the WISC with the general factor at time I and time II in the working-class and the middle-class areas.

TABLE 7.16 WISC *sub-tests and teachers' ratings (first principal component) within* LEA

	Verbal		*Performance*	
Working class	*Similarity*	*Vocabulary*	*Block design*	*Object assembly*
TR 1	0·313	0·518	0·363	0·410
TR 2	0·319	0·445	0·405	0·352
Middle class				
TR 1	0·350	0·229	0·133	0·120
TR 2	0·368	0·350	0·101	0·119
		Variances		
LEA	*Similarity*	*Vocabulary*	*Block design*	*Object assembly*
Working-class	9·481	10·666	11·071	7·041
Middle-class	8·147	7·027	9·142	5·645

We can see from Table 7.16 that at time I in the working-class area the correlation between the general factor and the similarity scale is 0·31, whereas the correlation between the vocabulary sub-scale and the general factor is 0·52. We have here some basis for the inference that teachers in the working-class area appear to be more sensitive to the child's *vocabulary* score than they are sensitive to the similarity score. We may note in passing that the correlation between the Crichton (which is also a vocabulary scale) and the general factor is virtually the same (0·52) as that of the WISC vocabulary scale. In the middle-class area at time I, the picture is reversed. The correlation between the *similarity scale* and the general factor is *higher* (0·35) than the correlation between the vocabulary scale (0·23) and the general factor. At time II in the working-class area, owing to relative movements, the difference between the similarity and vocabulary correlations with the general factor has become smaller, but it is still the case that the correlation between the vocabulary scale and the general factor is higher (0·45). In the middle-class area at time II, the correlation between the general factor and the vocabulary scale has increased from 0·23 to 0·35, and that between the similarity scale and the general factor has also risen, albeit slightly, from 0·35 to 0·37. If we now compare the position in the two areas at time II, it is still the case that in the working-class area the vocabulary scale still correlates more highly with the general factor than does any other sub-scale of the WISC; whereas in the middle-class area, it is the similarity scale which has the highest correlation with the general factor.

Summary

As a result of this evidence, the hypothesis presented earlier must be modified in the following respects:

1 At the *end of the first year*, there is strong evidence for the suggestion that in the middle-class area the teachers appear to be more sensitive to the operations underlying the similarity scale, and that in the working-class area the teachers appear to be more sensitive to word definition.

2 In the second year in the working-class area the correlation between the vocabulary scale and the general factor drops, but the vocabulary scale of the WISC still has the *highest* correlation with the general factor. The correlations between Crichton and the general factor is the highest of all tests, 0·53.

3 In the middle-class area in the second year, although the correlation between the vocabulary scale and the general factor has *increased*, the similarity scale still has the highest correlation with the general factor. The correlation between the Crichton and the general factor is 0·30.

4 There seems to be possibly the beginning of a trend towards the equal significance of *both* of the verbal sub-scales, but this movement is taking place more slowly in the working-class area.

5 It is quite clear that in the middle-class area the child's scores on the *performance scales of the* WISC bear little relation to the general factor. The teachers' judgements are only related to the child's verbal scores.

Conclusion

In the working-class area the vocabulary sub-scale has the highest correlation with the general factor at both time I and time II. In the middle-class area, the similarity sub-scale has the highest correlation with the general factor at both time I and time II. *Relatively, vocabulary is more important in the working-class area and similarity is more important in the middle-class area.* We consider that this analysis offers some support for the hypothesis of the relative significance for the teacher of analogical reasoning on the part of the child in the middle-class area.

In the working-class area, the communication structure within the family may give rise to a weaker differentiation of what count as educationally relevant abilities and competencies. This could explain the much higher correlations between verbal and performance tests in the working-class area. It appears that the teachers' focus in the verbal area is upon *descriptive* vocabulary. The cognitive orientations of the teachers in the two areas appear to be different. Previous results have shown that the teachers in the working-class areas are relatively less interested in the 'Independence' of the child, and are more interested in 'Co-operativeness' and 'Attentiveness'.

Chapter 8 Summary of the major findings: Part I and Part II

Part I

1 The approach

After a general review of the data matrix the rating-questionnaire is examined, and it is observed that most of the rating-questions contain a substantial prescriptive component as well as a descriptive one. Although the analysis of the ratings begins without any specific theoretical referents, the study is given a focus through the use of rating-scores, not as a description of the children rated but as a description of the teachers who do the rating. The strategy of analysis is to examine (i) the one-year stability of each rating-question across teachers, (ii) the structure of the rating-set, and (iii) the prediction of rating-scores from characteristics which the child brings to school.

2 Stability of teachers' ratings

The mean one-year stability between teachers is much higher for 'Brightness' and 'Future school career' than for the other ratings. Moreover, the stability and the variance of these two rating-questions vary rather less than those of other rating-questions, although it is also inferred that the variation of rating-variance is in part contingent on both the form of the rating-question and on its position in the rating-questionnaire. It is concluded that the teachers achieve much greater consensus when rating children on the more academic criteria.

3 Structure of the rating-set

The correlations between different rating-questions are generally high, and this may in part be attributed to a halo effect. It is argued that a substantial halo effect must be present because of the general value-bias in the rating-questionnaire, and that this halo effect will be a powerful influence on the first (i.e. general) factor in the rating-set. A decision is made to extract the first (and second) principal components from each teacher's rating-set, both in order to obtain some notion of the character of the halo effect, and, subsequently, to control for that effect in a study of individual rating-questions.

On average, the first principal component dominates the rating-set, and its composition suggests that it is indeed a predominantly halo-effect factor. Moreover, the stability of the first principal component is consistently very high, and this is so despite the fact that the first factor loadings of particular rating-questions vary considerably between teachers. However, the loadings of 'Brightness' and 'Future school career' vary much less than those of other ratings, and on average they are also clearly higher than those of the other ratings, despite some definite variability between times and LEAS in the character of the first principal component. From this it is deduced that the halo effect which is construed as shaping the first principal component revolves primarily around academic criteria.

4 Prediction of teachers' ratings

In order to predict children's rating-scores on the first principal component, a few major pre-school attributes are chosen for study: sex, social class, three IQ tests and an Index of Communication and Control (ICC). All these attributes make a significant contribution to the prediction of teachers' ratings in all or part of the sample. Given occasional statistical controls, there are no significant differences between individual teachers in the weight that they give to specific child-attributes, but there are some powerful differences between groups of teachers. In particular, the middle-class LEA teachers rate girls much more highly than boys, but give no weight at all to ICC, whereas the working-class LEA teachers rate high ICC children very highly, but give no significant overall weight to sex. In general, however, it is IQ, especially verbal IQ, which has the most powerful influence on teachers' ratings in both LEAS.

Some of these relationships are also weakly apparent in predicting the second principal component, as a result of which it is suggested (note 4) that a small orthogonal rotation of the first two principal components would have corrected for the inferred value-bias in the second component. Finally, the first principal component relationships are faithfully mirrored in the correlations between child-attributes and specific rating-questions.

The appendix to Chapter 4 goes on to explore the pattern of relationships between child attributes and teachers' ratings with the first principal component partialled out.

5 Teachers' ratings and intelligence

The dominance of IQ in predicting teachers' ratings suggests that the IQ-rating relationship deserves a fuller and more controlled exploration. This is done by setting up a grid of six variables: one first- and one second-year score to measure each of verbal IQ, non-verbal IQ and teachers' ratings. The correlations between these six variables in both LEAS suggests that the most powerful measure of general IQ in the three groups of variables is the teachers' ratings. This inference is given a more formal character by applying the bi-factor method to the correlation matrix. The ensuing discussion assigns equal sociological status to IQ tests and teachers' ratings, and concludes that if the 'modes of selection' controversy were introduced to the infant school, the final outcome would be no discernible effect on the kind of children selected.

Part II

The analysis in Part II was based upon a grouping of the data so as to reveal what were taken to be underlying trends. Although some of the differences do not quite reach statistical significance, the overall relational patterns seemed to the author to warrant often detailed discussion.

1 At the end of the first year the data suggest that in the working-class area the teacher's model of the 'successful' infant-school child stresses teacher-controlling or teacher-focusing behaviour. In the middle-class area, the data suggest that here the teacher's model of the 'successful' infant-school child stresses about equally teacher-controlling/focusing behaviour *and* pupil-initiating behaviour.

2 At the end of the second year, there are changes in the relative emphasis of components of the model of the 'successful' infant-school child in *both* areas. There is some indication, that in the working-class area there is relatively a greater stress on pupil-initiating behaviour, although 'Answering' (excluding the intellectual ratings) has by far the highest correlation with the general factor. Further, in the working-class area, at the end of the second year, there is a strengthening of the correlations between 'Explanation , 'Questioning' and 'Co-operativeness' and 'Attentiveness'; that is, a *strengthening* of the relationship between pupil-initiating and teacher-controlling behaviour. However, in the middle-class area there is considerable weakening of the above relationship. Further, in the middle-class area, if we exclude the intellectual ratings of 'Brightness' and 'Future school career', the rating which shows the *highest* correlation with the general factor is 'Independence'. In the working-class area, this rating shows only the *fourth* highest correlation with the general factor, and it occupies the *same* position in the second year as it does in the first year. The rating 'Independence' in the middle-class area has shifted dramatically from the fifth place to *first* place in order of the strength of correlation with the general factor. We also noted that in the middle-class area the child who was rated highly on 'Explanation' in the first year, is in the second year likely to be rated highly on 'Independence' and on 'Future school career', even though the correlation between 'Explanation' and the general factor in the second year has suffered a statistically significant reduction. In general, we would argue that in the middle-class area, relative to the working-class area, the infant-school pupils are expected to be self-regulating whereas in the working-class area they are more teacher-regulated. However, the emphasis in the middle-class area is itself based upon an initial sharing between teachers and infant pupils of the rules of appropriate conduct. In the working-class area, it seems that the pupils are less likely to find their spontaneous classroom behaviour rated highly until it has been subject to teacher regulation. In the contemporary jargon, the working-class pupil has to learn what counts as acceptable conduct.

3 Sex and teachers' ratings. In the middle-class area girls receive significantly higher ratings than do boys, so much so that the relationship between the sex of the child and the general factor is as *high* as the relationship between IQ and the general factor. In the working-class area the sex of the child in the first year has little relationship to the individual ratings. In the second year, girls are rated relatively more highly than boys on 'Explanation', 'Questioning', 'Attentiveness' and 'Co-operativeness', but the correlation between sex and the general factor at the end of the second year is still relatively small and reaches only the 0·05 level of significance.

4 Social class and teachers' ratings. Despite the greater social-class variance in the middle-class area, the correlations between the social-class background of the child and the general factor is *smaller* in the middle-class area than in the working-class area. Indeed, by the end of the second year there is *no* relation between the social-class background of the child and the general factor. In the working-class area the social-class background of the child at both time I and time II is related to the general factor. However, because the school class is the basic unit for analysis, and because the social composition of

each school class is relatively homogeneous, the correlations with social class are low.

5 Index of Communication and Control and teachers' ratings. In the middle-class area, as expected, there is no relationship between the ICC and the general factor. There is some suggestion, however, that in the middle-class area mothers who score high on the ICC have children who are viewed somewhat unfavourably by the teachers. In the working-class area, there is a strong relationship between the ICC and the general factor. Further, the rise in the correlation between the ICC and the general factor between time I and time II is greater than the increase in the relationship between IQ and the general factor. There is then some suggestion that the effects of the communication process in the working-class families may increase as the child gets older, *given* existing educational practice. In the working-class area, there is a sharp rise in the correlations between the ICC and the following individual ratings at the end of the second year: 'Questioning', 'Answering' and 'Co-operativeness'. It is of some interest that this measure of reported maternal communication and control obtained *before* the child went to school is increasingly related to the teachers' judgments of the child's *verbal* behaviour at the end of the child's second year in the infant school. There is a hint that high ICC scores call out different judgments of the teachers in the working-class and middle-class area. This would seem to imply that mothers with high ICC scores within the working-class area are not necessarily middle-class in their orientation.

6 In general, IQ is much *less* closely related to the general factor in the middle-class area. It is also the case that the relationships between IQ and the *individual* ratings is more extensive in the working-class than in the middle-class area. Further, the *non-verbal* IQ measures (particularly the performance scales of the WISC) are *much more* highly correlated with the general factor in the *working-class area* than in the middle-class area.

Polarisation of children in terms of measured ability is relatively much sharper in the working-class area than in the middle-class area, and this process is at work from the child's initial experience of school.

It is the case that the inter-correlations between verbal and non-verbal tests is very much higher in the working-class area than in the middle-class area, and it is this which is responsible for the stronger relationship between almost all the IQ tests and the general factor in the working-class area. The data further suggest that teachers in the working-class area are *relatively* more sensitive to vocabulary scales whereas teachers in the middle-class area are more sensitive to the similarity scales. We have interpreted this finding as indicating that teachers in the working-class area are rather more concerned with discriminatory choice of words (vocabulary). *If* the *statistical* relationships were to be borne out by observational studies of teachers' infant-school practice, then different cognitive attributes are being selectively developed in the two areas.

7 The background variables and the teachers' ratings. In the middle-class area only *two* background variables at the end of the second year relate to the teachers' ratings; sex and IQ and both of these are relatively small. In the working-class area *every* background variable at different strengths is related to the ratings: class, sex, IQ and ICC. However, it is *measured ability* which has the strongest relationship followed by the ICC which itself correlates with measured ability. This suggests that there is a process of selective preferment of children based upon measured ability and familial processes of communication which starts at five years of age and ends as a self-fulfilling prophesy.

8 In general, the findings suggest that teachers in these two areas are operating with different principles of control and selection which in their turn create criteria of conduct and competency which the children are expected to realise. And these differences are at work from the beginnings of the child's initial experience of the school.

9 We should like to repeat that these results and inferences are *no* criticism of the teachers; if anything they point to the more pervasive institutional constraints upon families, schools and educational practice.

Appendix The preparation of the infant-school child

by Jean Jones and Basil Bernstein

Introduction

We shall give in this appendix the mothers' answers to questions on the first questionnaire, which give some idea of the differences between the social classes as these refer to:

1 The nursery-school attendance of the child.
2 The expectation of the child adjusting favourably to the infant school.
3 The relationships between mothers and teachers.
4 The preparation of the child for the infant school.
5 The mothers' concepts of 'play' and 'work' and how they saw the relationship between the two.
6 The significant attributes of toys.
7 Membership of library by mother and child.
8 The reading pattern in the home.
9 The functions of reading.
10 The diagnosis of the origins of a child's learning difficulties.

Although we are concerned here with what the mothers say, *not* what they do, their answers reveal differences in attitude, and differences in the range of strategies they *say* they might employ, which may well have a bearing upon the child's response to the early years in the infant school. If the mothers' replies do reflect something of what they do, then there are major social-class differences in the socialisation of the child into the infant school.

Sample

The total number of mothers on whom we have some data is 473. However, as we interviewed the mothers before the child went to school, we have a slightly larger sample of mothers than we have of children, because by the September some of the children did not go to the sample schools.

Table A2.1 sets out the construction of the sample.

TABLE A2.1

Sample Size	*Total*	*W.I.*	*Remainder*	*Faulty tapes*	*Final sample*
Total children	473				
Twins	9				
Total mothers	464	23	441		
3 control schools	72	5	67		
15 remaining schools	392	18	374		
Refused interview	13	3	10		
Fully interviewed	379	15	364	4	360

Social-class index

A detailed discussion of the construction of this index is given in Appendix I by W. Brandis, in *Social Class, Language and Communication*, by W. Brandis and D. Henderson (1970). We have here used a collapsed form of the original ten-point scale. We have distinguished a middle-class, mixed class and working class.

Middle class (*n* = 110)

The parents of these families would be classified as 1, 2 or 3 on the Brandis scale of social class; nearly all parents in this group on the Hall-Jones scale would be classified as 1, 2, 3 or 4 and *all* received a selective education.

Working class (*n* = 126)

The parents of these families would be classified on the Brandis scale of social class as 7, 8 or 9; nearly all the parents in this group would be classified on the Hall-Jones scale as 5, 6 or 7 and *all* received a non-selective education.

Mixed class (*n* = 124)

The parents of these families would be classified on the Brandis scale of social class as 4, 5 or 6 *and* there is a tendency for there to be a discrepancy between occupational and educational status. This group is literally a mixed group.

Presentation of data

The tables we present have, for reasons of space, been given in a condensed form. Thus Table A2.2 (given as an example) should be interpreted as follows:

TABLE A2.2

	Working class	*Mixed*	*Middle class*	*n*	*Total*
%	60	40	20	148	360

60 per cent (76) of the working-class group made this response; 40 per cent (50) of the mixed-class group, and 20 per cent (22) of the middle-class group. In all, 148 out of the total sample of 360 offered this response.

Preparation of the child for school

We shall start off by considering how many of the sample children had attended a nursery school.

TABLE A2.3

	Working class	*Mixed*	*Middle class*	*n*	*Total*
%	22	31	57	129	360
					$\chi^2 = 33{\cdot}58$ $p = <0{\cdot}001$

We can see immediately from Table A2.3 that two-and-a-half times as many middle-class children had attended nursery schools than had working-class children. Over half the middle-class children had had this fortunate experience. It is unnecessary to comment on this result. It might be of interest to place next to this result the mother's expectation of the child's adjustment to school. All mothers were asked, 'After —— has been at school for a while, do you think you'll see any changes in him/her?' We analysed the mothers' replies to see whether they thought the child would adjust or have difficulty in adjusting to school (see Table A2.4).

TABLE A2.4 *Expectation that the child will adjust favourably to school*

	Working class	*Mixed*	*Middle class*	*n*	*Total*
%	29	27	44	118	360
					$\chi^2 = 33{\cdot}58$ $p = <0{\cdot}001$

We find that nearly half of the middle-class mothers thought their child would adjust favourably to school, whereas the percentage of both mothers of working-class and mixed class who were as optimistic is significantly much lower.

We will now present findings (Table A2.5) which give some impression of how the mothers see their relationship to the teacher. We asked, 'Is there anything a mother can do to make a teacher's job easier?' We analysed the mothers' replies into three broad groups. The first group consisted of replies in which the mothers stated they would prepare the child in some way for school. They mentioned the importance of the initial preparation of the child. The second group consisted of replies where the mothers stated that in some way they would help or support the teacher. The third group consisted of replies where the mothers indicated that they would give some information to the teacher about the child.

The vertical columns do not add up to 100 because some mothers gave more than one reason. We can see that, on the whole, the

TABLE A2.5 *Mother-teacher relationship*

	Working class	*Mixed*	*Middle class*	*n*
Prepares the child	% 41	53	68	192
Supports the teacher	% 14	61	40	89
Gives information about child	% 50	36	11	119

$\chi^2 = 18{\cdot}11$ $p = <0{\cdot}001$
$\chi^2 = 23{\cdot}51$ $p = <0{\cdot}001$
$\chi^2 = 41{\cdot}41$ $p = <0{\cdot}001$

middle-class mothers, relative to other mothers, talked about preparing the child and supporting the teacher. We can see, if we read the table vertically, that working-class mothers were very evenly split between preparing the child and giving information to the teacher about the child. Their replies were far less concerned with supporting the teacher. It might be reasonable to infer that they were more concerned about their child at school, and wanted the teacher to have some understanding/information about him. This would seem to underline the importance of home-school relationships developing very early in the child's primary-school life.

The question that we have just discussed came very late in the interview with the mother (question 20). The following questions were questions 3 and 4. We hoped that these questions would encourage the mothers to talk about how they would prepare the child for school.

> 'Do you think it is necessary for a parent to see the teacher before a child starts school?' (If YES is the only response, ask about what? If NO is the only response, ask 'Is there nothing much to talk about then?')
> 'What do you think a mother can tell a child about school, so that he/she will know what to expect?'

We shall first present an analysis of the mothers' replies in terms of the number of mothers in each social class who mentioned three, two, one or no acts of preparation.

We can see that, in terms of what the mothers said (*which might be different from what they actually do*), there are strong class differences in the range of preparatory acts (see Table A2.6).

We will now look more closely at the types of preparations mentioned by the mothers. We classified the mothers' replies as follows:

1 The mother mentioned that she would familiarise herself with the school in some way (Table A2.7).

TABLE A2.6 *Number of different types of preparatory acts*

		Working class	*Mixed*	*Middle class*	*n*
3+	%	18	34	46	116
2	%	32	37	37	125
1	%	40	24	15	97
0	%	10	5	2	22
		126	124	110	360

$\chi^2 = 32{\cdot}64\ p = <0{\cdot}001$

2 The mother would tell the teacher something about the child (Table A2.8).
3 The mother mentioned similarities between home and school (Table A2.9).
4 The mother mentioned that she would prepare the child for active participation in the class (Table A2.10).
5 The mother mentioned that she would prepare the child for a more docile or passive relationship (Table A2.11).

TABLE A2.7 *Mother mentions she will familiarise herself with the school*

	Working class	*Mixed*	*Middle class*	*n*	*Total*
%	32	50	55	162	360
			$\chi^2 = 14{\cdot}24$ $p = < 0{\cdot}001$		

TABLE A2.8 *Mother will tell teacher something about the child*

	Working class	*Mixed*	*Middle class*	*n*	*Total*
%	29	27	29	102	360
				Not significant	

TABLE A2.9 *Mother mentions similarities between home and school*

	Working class	*Mixed*	*Middle class*	*n*	*Total*
%	4	9	16	34	360
			$\chi^2 = 12{\cdot}90$ $p = < 0{\cdot}01$		

TABLE A2.10 *Preparation of child for active role*

	Working class	*Mixed*	*Middle class*	*n*	*Total*
%	30	35	54	140	360
			$\chi^2 = 15{\cdot}01$ $p = < 0{\cdot}001$		

TABLE A2.11 *Preparation of child for passive role*

	Working class	*Mixed*	*Middle class*	*n*	*Total*
%	31	20	12	77	360
			$\chi^2 = 12{\cdot}90\ p = <0{\cdot}01$		

First of all, we can see that over one-third of all the mothers mentioned something about familiarising themselves with the school, telling the teacher something about the child and preparing the child for active participation in the school class. ('There are lots of things to do.') It is also the case that the working-class mothers lay relatively less stress on an active relationship and familiarising themselves with the school, and relatively more stress on preparing the child for a more passive role ('Do what the teacher says'). However, Table A2.10 indicates that nearly one-third of the working-class mothers did mention that they would prepare the child for active participation in the infant-school class. From what the mothers *said* it would seem that the range of preparatory acts is related to the social-class position of the family, and that there are social-class differences in the type of preparation.

We will now look at the mothers' attitudes to the content of infant school education.

Play

All mothers were asked the following question. 'Some people think that for the first couple of years at school, children spend most of their time playing while other people think they start working much too soon. How do you feel about this?'

TABLE A2.12 *Time limit required on play*

	Working class	*Mixed*	*Middle class*	*n*	*Total*
%	52	40	34	152	360
			$\chi^2 = 8{\cdot}00\ p = <0{\cdot}02$		

The question was deliberately worded so that the mothers would talk about their ideas of 'play' and 'work'. We were very interested to find out whether mothers understood the educational significance of 'play'. We were also concerned to see how they would strike the balance between 'work' and 'play'. The mothers interpreted work in terms of basic skills: reading, arithmetic, writing.

Table A2.12 indicates that 52 per cent of the working-class mothers said they would prefer and like to see some time limit on play activities, whereas the percentage of the mixed and middle-class mothers who explicitly referred to such a limit is significantly less.

TABLE A2.13 *Positive attitude to basic skills*

	Working class	*Mixed*	*Middle class*	*n*	*Total n*
%	46	59	61	197	360
			$\chi^2 = 7{\cdot}13$ $p = <0{\cdot}05$		

We can see from Table A2.13 that nearly two-thirds of the sample mentioned the importance of basic skills, but there is a small but significant increase in the percentage of the mixed and middle-class mothers who mentioned the importance of basic skills.

TABLE A2.14 *Positive attitude to play*

	Working class	*Mixed*	*Middle class*	*n*	*Total n*
%	27	22	55	121	360
			$\chi^2 = 31{\cdot}84$ $p = <0{\cdot}001$		

The result in Table A2.14 shows that a much smaller percentage of the total sample *mentioned* that they approved of play as compared with the percentage of the total sample who mentioned the importance of basic skills: 121 (play): 197 (basic skills). Of the mothers who held a positive attitude to play, a far greater percentage of middle-class mothers held this attitude than either mothers in the mixed class or working-class.

TABLE A2.15 *Play seen as educationally significant*

	Working class	*Mixed*	*Middle class*	*n*	*Total n*
%	12	10	44	75	360
			$\chi^2 = 49{\cdot}84$ $p = <0{\cdot}001$		

We can see that only just under one-*fifth* of the total sample actually mentioned the educational value of play (Table A2.15), but nearly one half of these were middle-class mothers. ('It's not really play, is it?')

TABLE A2.16 *Balance required between play and work*

	Working class	*Mixed*	*Middle class*	*n*	*Total*
%	17	30	62	125	360
			$\chi^2 = 54{\cdot}84$ $p = <0{\cdot}001$		

Nearly one-third of the sample (Table A2.16) indicated that there should be a balance between these two activities but 62 per cent of the middle-class mothers indicated this.

In general, and as to be expected, the middle-class mothers were more favourably disposed to play and a greater percentage of these mothers mentioned its educational importance, but a much higher percentage of the middle-class mothers wanted to see some kind of balance between work and play. Nearly two-thirds of the sample stressed the importance of basic skills and only between one-third and just under one-fifth indicated a favourable attitude to play and some, albeit minimum, recognition of the educational significance of play.

Attributes of toys

At this point, it might be useful to turn to the mothers' attitudes to toys. We were concerned with this area because not only are toys a source of potential learning, but it is also important to understand how the mothers see toys in relation to the child. The mothers were asked, 'What do you look out for if you're buying a toy as a present for a child your son's or daughter's age?' (We are referring here to a child about five years of age.)

We classified the mothers' replies as follows:

1 Some reference to the age or sex of the child (Table A2.17).
2 Some reference to the physical properties of toys (Table A2.18).
3 Some reference to educational aspects (Table A2.19).
4 Some reference to the explorative/imaginative aspect (Table A2.20).
5 Some reference to the child's own preference (Table A2.21).
6 Some reference to the social aspect, i.e. playing with other children (Table A2.22).
7 Some reference to toys as assisting the child's development (Table A2.23).
8 Some reference to the value of the toy for the mother (keep him amused, quiet, etc) (Table A2.24).

TABLE A2.17 *Age and sex considered*

	Working class	*Mixed*	*Middle class*	*n*	*Total*
%	9	14	42	74	360
			$\chi^2 = 44{\cdot}77$ $p = <0{\cdot}001$		

TABLE A2.18 *Physical property considered*

	Working class	*Mixed*	*Middle class*	*n*	*Total*
%	34	30	46	130	360
			$\chi^2 = 6{\cdot}46$ $p = <0{\cdot}05$		

TABLE A2.19 *Some reference to educational aspect*

	Working class	*Mixed*	*Middle class*	*n*	*Total*
%	27	30	36	109	360
				Not significant	

TABLE A2.20 *Some reference to explorative/imaginative aspect*

	Working class	*Mixed*	*Middle class*	*n*	*Total*
%	22	39	44	124	360
				$\chi^2 = 13{\cdot}43$ $p = <0{\cdot}01$	

TABLE A2.21 *Some reference to child's own preferences*

	Working class	*Mixed*	*Middle class*	*n*	*Total*
%	50	56	46	181	360
				Not significant	

TABLE A2.22 *Some reference to social aspect* (playing with other children)

	Working class	*Mixed*	*Middle class*	*n*	*Total*
%	10	5	6	25	360
				Not significant	

TABLE A2.23 *Some reference to the child's development*

	Working class	*Mixed*	*Middle class*	*n*	*Total*
%	1	2	18	23	360
				$\chi^2 = 31{\cdot}67$ $p = <0{\cdot}001$	

TABLE A2.24 *Some reference to value for the mother* ('keeps him amused, quiet')

	Working class	*Mixed*	*Middle class*	*n*	*Total*
%	8	5	4	20	360
				Not significant	

We can see that the aspects most frequently mentioned were the physical, educational, explorative aspects and, of course, reference to what the child wanted. It is also of interest that when the question is put in this way, the middle class do not spontaneously mention more frequently the educational aspects than either of the mixed or working class. The major class difference is found in the exploring/imaginative aspect. The working-class mothers mention this much less frequently, although again we must point out that 22 per cent of the mothers do refer to this aspect. Very few mothers mentioned the developmental aspect (23), but within this group it is a reply far more typical of the middle-class mother. Clearly views on toys are affected by exposure to journals, books, radio, TV and certain newspapers. We also classified the toys the mothers mentioned into ones which appeared to us as possibly emphasising cognitive, creative, role-playing, mechanical possibilities. There were no class differences on the type of toy mentioned.

Finally, we counted the number of aspects of toys the mothers mentioned, and examined social-class differences in the range (Table A2.25).

TABLE A2.25 *Number of aspects*

	Working class	*Mixed*	*Middle class*	*n*
0–3	84	74	48	254
3–5	16	26	52	106
		$\chi^2 = 32{\cdot}4\ p = <0{\cdot}001$		

Middle-class mothers mentioned a greater number of different aspects. Before we leave this area, it is worthwhile mentioning that later in the interview the mothers were asked to rank in order of importance six different usages of toys. As this has been reported elsewhere (Bernstein and Young, 1967) we shall give here one of the major findings. Middle-class mothers ranked higher the statement 'To find out about things' than did mothers in the other social-class groups (compare with Table A2.20).

Reading

We shall now consider the question of reading. We asked the mothers questions about library membership, how often they read to their child, and a further question which attempted to encourage the mother to talk about the function of reading. The functions of reading question was number 28 in the interview, reading frequency was number 29, and library membership was numbers 30 and 31. We will look first at library membership (see Tables A2.26 and A2.27).

TABLE A2.26 *Membership of library by the mother*

	Working class	*Mixed*	*Middle class*	*n*	*Total*
%	9	39	75	142	360
					$\chi^2 = 62{\cdot}53$ $p = <0{\cdot}001$

TABLE A2.27 *Membership of library by sample child*

	Working class	*Mixed*	*Middle class*	*n*	*Total*
%	25	48	80	179	360
					$\chi^2 = 72{\cdot}22$ $p = <0{\cdot}001$

It is of some interest that more working-class children belong to a library than do working-class mothers. It is also very clear that there is an enormous difference between the classes in terms of library membership of either mother or child. *In order to clarify the finding we should also have asked, 'How near is the library to your home?' and, 'How often do you go?'*

We will now give the results of the following questions. 'Does anyone in your family have much time to read to ——?' 'How often?' In Table A2.28 we give the results for where the mother mentioned that reading was a frequent activity, or where it was clear that there was a fixed pattern.

TABLE A2.28 *Mother indicates that child is read to frequently*

	Working class	*Mixed*	*Middle class*
%	19	36	71
			$\chi^2 = 66{\cdot}99$ $p = <0{\cdot}001$

Finally, we will examine differences in the functions of reading. We asked the mothers the following question. Here are some reasons mothers have given for reading to their children:

1 It helps them to go to sleep.
2 It is a quiet time for mother and child during the day.
3 It increases the number of words they know.
4 It is a way of occupying children when they can't go out to play.

We then said, 'Do you agree with these?' 'Is there anything else you think is more important?'

We asked the question in this way because we wanted the mothers to tell us what *they* thought was important. Table A2.29 gives the number of mothers in each social class who did not go beyond the four measures given above; that is, they did not mention that anything else was more important.

TABLE A2.29

	Working class	*Mixed*	*Middle class*	*n*	*Total*
%	71	55	34	194	360
					$\chi^2 = 32{\cdot}40\ p = <0{\cdot}001$

We then analysed what the mothers thought was more important than the original reasons. From Table A2.29, we can see that 29 per cent, 45 per cent and 66 per cent of the mothers (respectively working class, mixed and middle class) went on to give reasons. We classified the mothers' further reasons in the following way:

1 *Inter-actional* (Table A2.30)
e.g. 'Mother and child are together for a while.'
'It comforts the child.'
'It shows him I care for him.'
2 *Instrumental skills* (Table A2.31)
e.g. 'Helps him to learn to read.'
'Teaches him how to recognise words.'
'Teaches him to concentrate.'
3 *Cognitive* (Table A2.32)
e.g. 'Helps the child to learn about/find out about things.'
4 *Explorative/imaginative* (Table A2.33)
e.g. 'It stimulates the child.'
'It feeds his imagination.'

TABLE A2.30 *Inter-actional*

	Working class	*Mixed*	*Middle class*	*n*	*Total*
%	9	16	23	56	360
				$\chi^2 = 8{\cdot}78$ $p = <0{\cdot}02$	

TABLE A2.31 *Instrumental skills*

	Working class	*Mixed*	*Middle class*	*n*	*Total*
%	10	14	23	54	360
				$\chi^2 = 8{\cdot}78$ $p = <0{\cdot}02$	

TABLE A2.32 *Cognitive*

	Working class	*Mixed*	*Middle class*	*n*	*Total*
%	10	19	33	72	360
				$\chi^2 = 18{\cdot}65$ $p = <0{\cdot}001$	

TABLE A2.33 *Explorative/imaginative*

	Working class	*Mixed*	*Middle class*	*n*	*Total*
%	3	11	23	42	360
				$\chi^2 = 23{\cdot}60$ $p = <0{\cdot}001$	

As mothers gave more than one function, the numbers do not necessarily add up to the numbers in each social class. Of the mothers who went on to give further reasons, more mothers gave replies which could be classified as 'cognitive'. This function is most pronounced amongst the middle-class mothers. The social-class differences in functions of reading are strongest in the case of cognitive and explorative/imaginative functions.

According to the above findings, there are major differences between the social classes in the general area of books, reading and their functions.

Learning difficulties

Finally, we shall examine the replies the mothers gave to questions about the learning difficulties children might have at school.

'Not often, but sometimes, a child doesn't seem to learn at school – why do you think this is?'

'If this happens, what can a mother do?' (Questions 8, 8a).

'At what age should a mother start thinking about her child's progress at school?' (Question 10).

'Do you think a mother can help, or do anything about this?' (Question 10a).

Question 10 was asked in order to move on to the major question which followed (10a).

We analysed the answers to the first question first of all in terms of the number of influential factors (home, child, school) and then we carried out a more detailed analysis of each particular area of influence.

TABLE A2.34 *Number of influential factors mentioned*

	Working class	*Mixed*	*Middle class*	*n*
One	68	51	43	196
Two or Three	27	44	50	144
			$\chi^2 = 18{\cdot}86\ p = <0{\cdot}01$	

We can see from Table A2.34 that working-class mothers were more likely to mention only one influential factor. We shall now give a more detailed account of the replies. We shall first give the family, as on the whole there were relatively few mentions of the family as an influential factor. We had prepared a very delicate set of codes for this factor, but, because of the relatively few remarks, we distinguished between any comments about the degree of interest of the family in education, and any comments to do with the child's relationships with other members of the family.

Although the figures in Table A2.35 are very small, there is a suggestion that the middle-class mothers, relative to other mothers, were more likely to mention aspects of the relationships between members

TABLE A2.35 *Source of influence: the family*

	Working class	Mixed	Middle class	*n*
Concern with education	% 10	8	3	26
Relationships within the family	% 6	9	16	37

$\chi^2 = 5{\cdot}20$ Not significant
$\chi^2 = 6{\cdot}82\ p = <0{\cdot}05$

TABLE A2.36 *Source of influence: the child*

	Working class	Mixed	Middle class	*n*
Attitudes to learning	% 49	43	39	158
Cognitive orientation	% 20	38	46	123
Psychological difficulties	% 18	21	36	89
Relationship to the teacher	% 10	17	21	57

$\chi^2 = 2{\cdot}55$ Not significant
$\chi^2 = 19{\cdot}70\ p = <0{\cdot}001$
$\chi^2 = 11{\cdot}80\ p = <0{\cdot}01$
$\chi^2 = 6{\cdot}50\ p <0{\cdot}05$

of the family as having some bearing upon the child's learning difficulties.

Table A2.36 shows that there were no social-class differences in the child's attitudes to learning. We coded under this category any mention of the child being bored, inattentive, distractable, lazy. There are social-class differences in cognitive orientation, psychological difficulties and relationship to the teacher. Cognitive orientation of the child refers to brightness, problems of understanding and also to the child's developmental stage (i.e. 'Some children are late starters, aren't they?'). Psychological difficulties refers to an emotional problem or disturbance, anxiety/worry, problems in mixing with other children, or unhappiness ('He was just unhappy'). Relationship to the teacher refers specifically to the child not getting on with the teacher, or the teacher not getting on with the child. The clearest social-class *trend* appears in the categories of psychological difficulties and cognitive orientation.

TABLE A2.37 *Source of influence: the school*

		Working class	*Mixed*	*Middle class*	*n*
General reference to school	%	3	7	10	24
Reference to teacher	%	18	22	17	69
Reference to size of class	%	13	17	27	67

$\chi^2 = 4{\cdot}50$ Not significant
$\chi^2 = 0{\cdot}80$ Not significant
$\chi^2 = 8{\cdot}50\ p = <0{\cdot}02$

We can see that in Table A2.37, there is only one significant difference; the middle-class mothers were more likely to refer to the size of the class as a factor in the child's learning difficulty. In general then, the middle-class mothers *mention* a greater range of influences upon the child and *mention* more frequently learning difficulties which arise out of inter-personal relationships in the family, psychological difficulties in the child, relationships to the teacher, and size of class.

Conclusions

We must underline that the evidence we have presented is based upon what mothers said in a tape-recorded interview. This is not the place to go into the training of the interviewers, the initial approaches to the mother and the conduct of the interview, as a very full report of this is available in the SRU monograph, *Social Control and Socialization* by Jenny Cook-Gumperz (1973). We should bear in mind that different mothers react differently to a context where they are asked a range of questions in an inter-action where there is, *during* the questions, a limited amount of uncontrolled dialogue. There is also the issue as to whether the mothers discussed the areas covered in the family, with other mothers, or with teachers. Finally, it is also the case that what a mother says is not necessarily what she does and what a mother does not say is no necessary indication of what she does not do. In the same way, what she thinks is not necessarily what she says. We should, however, point out that the mothers were interviewed twice during the research, and the second interview did cover some of the same ground as the first. We also have been able to show relationships between what the mothers said and the behaviour of the child in another situation.

The results point to the following issues:

1 The relationship to the school should be such that mothers feel they can make an effective contribution to their child's experience in the classroom. This underlines the need for the early establishment of home/school relationships so that the mother (parents) can find out and also actively consider what goes on.
2 Shifts in educational practice are not necessarily matched by parallel shifts in parental knowledge or approval.
3 Given the emphasis upon reading, the results support the view that this problem has *one* of its *many* roots in class-related differences in the definition of and orientation towards books and reading.
4 The middle-class mothers appear to be able to consider a wider range of influences and appear to be able to adopt a wider range of strategies of educational relevance to their children.
5 The data we have presented here and the results of the second interview indicate the fundamental incorrectness of the view that working-class mothers are not interested or concerned about their child's life in school. Nearly half the working-class mothers wanted to be able to give some information to the teacher about their child; half of the working-class mothers wanted a time limit on play and stressed the importance of basic skills. These mothers would feel encouraged rather than compensated if the nursery school provision was such that 57 per cent of their children (like the middle class) could go to one. It would not be presumptuous to suggest that they would be delighted to have the same housing resources as the middle-class mothers, equivalent facilities, educational resources, time and income. Would they not like to have the possibility mentioned by 62 per cent of the middle-class mothers of removing their child from the school if the child was not making the progress they would like to see? It may be that only 29 per cent of the working-class mothers mentioned this alternative because it was somewhat unrealistic. Social-class acts selectively and unequally on the distribution of what counts as valued resources, be they physical or symbolic.

These findings are in no way surprising because the overwhelming majority of readers of this book are aware of them. However, awareness has no inevitable correlation with adequate action. We are including this Appendix not because it has added anything to what is already known, but because it provides a background to how the teachers rated the children of these mothers at the end of the first and second year of their school life.

Bibliography

BERNSTEIN, B. and BRANDIS, W. (1970), 'Social class differences in communication and control', ch. 3, in Brandis, W. and Henderson, D. (1970).

BERNSTEIN, B. and HENDERSON, D. (1969), 'Social class differences in the relevance of language to socialisation', *Sociology*, 3, no. 1.

BERNSTEIN, B. and YOUNG, D. (1967), 'Social class differences in conceptions of the uses of toys', *Sociology*, vol. 1, no. 2; reprinted as ch. 1 in *Class, Codes and Control*, ed. B. Bernstein, vol. 2, Routledge & Kegan Paul, 1973.

BOX, G. E. P. (1950), 'Problems in the analysis of growth and wear curves', *Biometrics*, 6, 362–89.

BRANDIS, W. and HENDERSON, D. (1970), *Social Class, Language and Communication*, Routledge & Kegan Paul.

CATTELL, R. B. (1964), 'Validity and reliability: a proposed more basic set of concepts', *Journal of Educational Psychology*, 55, 1–22.

COOK-GUMPERZ, J. (1973), *Social Control and Socialization*, Routledge & Kegan Paul.

EDWARDS, A. L. (1968), *Experimental Design in Psychological Research*, Holt, Rinehart & Winston.

GAHAGAN, D. M. and GAHAGAN, G. A. (1970), *Talk Reform: Exploration in Language for Infant School Children*, Routledge & Kegan Paul.

HARMAN, H. H. (1967), *Modern Factor Analysis*, University of Chicago Press.

HENDERSON, D. (1970), 'Contextual specificity, discretion and cognitive socialisation: with special reference to language', *Sociology*, v. 2, no. 3.

INGLEBY, J. D. and COOPER, E. S. (1974), 'How teachers perceive first year school children: sex and ethnic differences', not yet published, M.R.C. Unit, London School of Economics.

JONES, J. (1966), 'Social class and the under-fives', *New Society*, 22 December.

MITCHELL, J. V., JR (1956), 'A comparison of the factorial structure of cognitive functions for a high and low status group', *Journal of Educational Research*, 47, 397–414.

ROBINSON, W. P. and RACKSTRAW, S. J. (1972). *A Question of Answers*, Routledge & Kegan Paul.

WINER, B. J. (1962), *Statistical Principles in Experimental Design*, McGraw-Hill.

Index